MW01286546

This exc[...]
for all who w[...]
counseling. I[...]
psychology, and on target in its direction [...]
biblical approach to counseling.

Dr. Jerry Vines
Pastor Emeritus,
First Baptist Church, Jacksonville, Florida
Two-time President,
Southern Baptist Convention

Dr. Paige Patterson has addressed the elephant in the room of pastoral counseling in his book, *The Sufficiency of the Bible in Counseling*. It is a well known part of pastoring that every pastor must give wise counsel to parishioners, but the dilemma is the source of the counseling. Well-meaning pastors, who claim the banner of inerrancy, have devoted many hours to secular thought when attempting to give counsel by those who promoted the antithesis of Christianity. B.F. Skinner and Sigmund Freud live in the world of secular thought and in the counseling sessions of good pastors. *The Sufficiency of the Bible in Counseling* sends the call for pastors and counselors to understand the role of the Bible and its clear teachings on anthropology, psychology, and human development. Dr. Patterson has accomplished a great service to the church in this book.

Dr. Marvin Jones
President,
Montana Christian College

Every minister is a minister of the Word of God. Whether delivered to the congregation or to an individual in counseling, the message delivered is a message from God! Thank you, Paige Patterson, for reminding us again of the centrality of the Word of God in the counseling ministry of the church.

Dr. Jimmy Draper
President Emeritus,
LifeWay

Every minister is a minister of the Word of God. With candor and conviction, Dr. Patterson challenges the church to be biblically literate when it comes to dealing with the matters of the soul. His premise that a believer equipped with his Bible is sufficient to disciple man towards personal holiness is refreshing in a culture where the Bible is devalued publicly and in the pulpits. I highly recommend this book to the body of Christ as a resource for helping believers navigate through the jungle of life.

Dr. Timothy Pigg
Pastor,
Fellowship Church, Immokalee/Ava Maria, FL

Is it possible for today's pastor to provide competent counseling to the members of his flock? Should counseling be left to psychologists, psychotherapists, and secular counselors? What should be the primary source of information for the pastor who attempts to counsel? Should the Bible be used in the counseling room? These questions and more are answered by Dr. Paige Patterson in the volume you hold in your hand. God's Word is sufficient! Pastors must reclaim their role of offering Biblical Counsel to the members of their flock. Every pastor should read this volume. Every believer should read this book as well. Now is the time for the church to recapture its role of Biblical Counseling.

Dr. Mark H. Ballard
President,
Northeastern Baptist College, Bennington, VT

The Sufficiency
of the Bible
in Counseling

The Sufficiency
of the Bible
in Counseling

Paige Patterson

NORTHEASTERN BAPTIST PRESS

Bennington, Vermont

TABLE OF CONTENTS

FOREWORD

by

Robert Jeffress

Dr. Paige Patterson's *The Sufficiency of the Bible in Counseling* is a much-needed reminder for the body of Christ about the power of God's Word. Although I certainly believe in the need for Christian psychiatrists and counselors to address some issues, the truth of God's Word should be the foundation for all counseling.

The church would be a healthier place mentally, emotionally, and spiritually if we would recognize once again the powerful role that Scripture should play in our lives. The Bible is "living and active and sharper than any two-edged sword, and piercing as far as the division of soul and spirit, of both joints and marrow, and able to judge the thoughts and intentions of the heart" (Hebrews 4:12). God's Word can cut right through us like a surgeon's scalpel. The Holy Spirit can work through it to give us a heart transplant, filling us with hope and healing we can find nowhere else.

This is why I think every believer, armed with the Word of God, has a vital role in bringing healing to those who are lost and hurting. The Bible alone cannot solve every problem. But the Bible alone has the answer to the most fundamental problem that plagues us all, our alienation from God by slavery to sin. Dr. Patterson convincingly argues that any therapeutic answer given without reference to the gospel will ultimately fail to bring full healing and joy.

Dr. Patterson is a gifted theologian, pastor, and leader. Over many decades of service to Christ, he has shown his fidelity to the inspired Word of God again and again. I hope that his words will receive a wide hearing in the church. I pray that his call would help spark a movement that makes the church once again a hospital for the hurting, bringing the hope and healing only Christ can bring!

Dr. Robert Jeffress
Senior Pastor,
First Baptist Church, Dallas, TX

Preface

An increasing number of voices have arisen from within the mental health industry concerning the paucity of scientific rigor in diagnosis and therapy. Rather than making an emotional response to the message of this book, why not consult some of these researchers, psychologists, and psychiatrists? You will find some of these published works cited in the annotated bibliography in the Appendix to this book.

The purpose of this slim volume is not to mount an assault on the psychiatric industry propped up by big Pharma. To the contrary, as a follower of Christ, I rejoice when anyone is permanently changed for the better by whatever means. Gracious women and men who love Christ devotedly labor in the healthcare arena to relieve emotional trauma in the lives of sufferers.

Christians are right, however, to insist that "soft sciences" like psychology produce the same evidence for verifying their claims and practices that are typical of a science like biology. When something cannot bear repeatability for verification, then call it a "theory" until it is verified. Also, many are rightly calling for significant reduction in the increased level of prescription drug use in the modern culture.

Nevertheless, the real burden of this book initially is to remind pastors, missionaries, and other faith practitioners that we are not trained to be physicians, psychiatrists, or pharmacologists. Rather than adopting the argot of the psychiatric professor or ceding the high calling of biblical counseling to "professionals," the church is challenged to take seriously its task of biblical guidance for life. A sympathetic, biblically-literate Christian is still the finest counselor available for other believers. Those who are not believers may also want to give these sensitive and caring encouragers a try since their effective methods are based on biblical truth.

God has not arbitrarily determined that some things are right, contributing to happiness and good relationships, while other things are wrong, leading to unhappiness and a breech in human relationships. Rather, God knows exactly the nature of those whom He has created–what behaviors and attitudes crown that creation. Those attitudes and actions that help are right. Those that diminish life are wrong. Who knows more about judging the difference than a biblically literate pastor or other God-anointed believer?

This book is a plea for the church again to function as a church. The duty of the church is not to interfere with what others may suggest, though we may have legitimate questions that need factual answers. Our province is rather faithfully to point out from Scripture what is revealed about the mind of God. What has God revealed to us about gender, sexual acts, sobriety, anger, race, justice, etc., *ad infinitum*? And once you know how God sees a matter, what are the steps you need to take to implement God's perspective, and what results can you expect in your own life? The deeply committed, thoroughly biblically-literate believer can do this one assignment of presenting God's truth with greater alacrity than even the most educated professional.

Read this short treatise with open mind and heart and see if God does not have the answers our world so desperately needs. Let the church be the church again.

CHAPTER 1

The Limitations of Freud and His Industry

Preoccupation with animals, especially canines, is a well-known disorder from which I have suffered all my life. To date I have not located this Disorder in the current *Diagnostic and Statistical Manual of Mental Disorders (DSM-5)*, but I am certain that it will make the DSM-6. Most probably it will be called Canine Disruptive Disorder. For an extended time, I ran Treeing Walker hounds, a uniquely-American breed tailored for hunting raccoons, bobcats, fox, and mountain lions. These dogs may be a little short on conventional canine grey matter, but they make up for that deficiency in courage, stamina, and the ability to climb trees. Two of these remarkable hounds, A. J. and the Bandit, were my companions at Southeastern Baptist Theological Seminary, where I served as President for more than a decade. Bandit did counseling with me, specializing in house calls to the dorms. A. J. was not much on counseling, preferring the role of prophet.

One day as I was walking through the campus, the dogs spotted a squirrel and pursued. A visiting family on campus missed the first part of the chase, but their seven-year-old son called attention to it upon discovering that the dogs had climbed the tree after the squirrel. "Look, Daddy, there is a dog in that tree," squealed the little boy with excitement.

Well, a father knows best, and he certainly knew that dogs do not climb trees. With a facial expression resembling an Atlantic hurricane, the father informed this little fellow, "If you do not stop dropping whoppers like that, I am going to wash your mouth out with detergent and warm your bottom to an unholy temperature."

That was my cue. "Sir," I said, "would you glance in the direction of the chapel and tell me what that is in the tree?" It would be inappropriate here to tell you precisely what this pre-seminarian uttered next, but I will tell you that he likely would not have said it in your church. Perhaps no blame should be assigned to this man. After all, he was guilty only of an exaggerated confidence in the "common core" of public wisdom, which would surely have argued that it is not scientifically possible for dogs to climb trees.

Little harm is done by believing that common core of wisdom regarding dogs and trees unless you happen to be a threatened little boy with a penchant for truth. But in America there is a "common core" of "wisdom" about the mental health industry that is exceedingly troubling. The tenacity with which it holds the public captive despite numerous skeptical books written from within its big pharmaceutical, multi-billion-dollar empire is more tenacious than the bite of my Walker hounds.

Problems with Conventional Wisdom

Peter Gotzsche focuses attention on the nature of the problem in his perceptive book, *Deadly Medicines and Organized Crime: How big pharma has corrupted healthcare*, when he notes:

> If we treat patients with depression in primary care with an antidepressant drug for 6 weeks, about 60% of them will improve. This seems like a good effect. However, if we treat the patients with a blinded placebo that looks just the same as the active pill, 50% of them will improve. Most doctors in-

terpret this as a large placebo effect, but it isn't possible to interpret the result in this way. If we don't treat the patients at all, but just see them again after 6 weeks, many of them will also have improved. We call this the spontaneous remission of the disease or its natural course.[1]

William Epstein, in the *Illusion of Psychotherapy*, is even less reticent when he says:

The voice of science in the psychotherapy community is weak, lacking any apparent influence over the quality of its research or the depth of its self-scrutiny. The scholarship of psychotherapy more resembles the intensely censored communication of cults than the open, direct, and tough cross-examining challenges that define intellectual exchanges between scholars committed to the canons of science. The field's poor research masks patient deterioration and protects its communal interests at the expense of the broader civic culture. Critical thought

---

1   Peter C. Gotzsche, *Deadly Medicines and Organized Crime: How big pharma has corrupted healthcare* (New York: Radcliffe, 2013), 43.

itself seems to have largely abandoned the therapeutic enterprise.[2]

Tana Dineen, borrowing the analogy of E. Fuller Torrey in his book *Witchdoctors and Psychiatrists*, said:

Torrey once described psychology as "the world's second oldest profession, remarkably similar to the first. Both involve a contract (implicit or explicit) between a specialist and a client for a service, and for this service a fee is paid."[107] Both professions shape themselves and their services to fit the wishes and feelings of their clients, to make them feel better in body or in mind, but the underlying goal is to do what ever [sic] has to be done in order to make a living. "Give the customer what he wants" is the motto, whether it is the pleasure of sex, the benefits of strong workers and soldiers, the thrill of self-actualization, or the blamelessness of victimhood. In this liaison, American society has abandoned its moral and cultural tradition while psychol-

2 William Epstein, *The Illusion of Psychotherapy* (New Brunswick, NJ: Transaction Publishers, 1995), 131.

ogy has lost its soul and neglected, even scorned, its own scientific foundation.[3]

But this book's purpose is not to call psychology to repentance even though I suspect this action is needed. I would exhort the practitioners of psychology and psychiatry to acknowledge their indebtedness to the atheistic philosophies of B. F. Skinner and Sigmund Freud, confess the limitations of the scientific foundation upon which they are constructed, and admit the degree to which, in some cases, the acquisition of money has motivated conclusions for what is one of the "soft sciences." If "psychology" lay prone on my office couch, lamenting the fact that he had become dysfunctional and felt somewhat unnerved by all this, I think that I would counsel "truth therapy." Just tell the truth, and you will feel better. So will the social order!

The purpose of this verbal adventure is to argue that the church should not abandon its birthright for a bowl of red psychotherapeutic pottage. Though I suspect that one can read the *Diagnostic and Statis-*

---

3 Tana Dineen, *Manufacturing Victims: What the Psychology Industry is Doing to People* (Westmount, QC: Robert Davies Multimedia, 1996), 132. Footnote 107 is cited from E. Fuller Torrey's *Witchdoctors and Psychiatrists* (see p. 138 in Dineen's volume). "Torrey, E. Fuller. *Witchdoctors and Psychiatrists*. New York: Harper and Row, 1986. p. 1."

tical Manual of Mental Disorders with the same profit obtained from a reading of *Bulfinch's Mythology*, I will leave the whole discussion of the reliability of the psychotherapeutic industry to better minds than my own.[4] What I do intend to attempt is to reassert that the ministry of counseling or pastoral ministries is still the task given to the church and not one to be abandoned without infinite spiritual devastation to the body of Christ.

THE BASIS FOR BIBLICAL COUNSELING

Four fundamental truths set the stage for Christian counseling. Though none of these will be a revelation to any of you, I do hope to arrange the information so as to underscore in a fresh way the authority and the confidence of the counselor.

The first fundamental truth of Christian counseling is predicated on the doctrine of creation. Genesis 1:1 declares that "In the beginning God

---

4 I have included at the end of this book an annotated bibliography of cogent publications for your convenience. This bibliography consists of books on psychology, psychiatry, and pharmacology written in most cases by secularists who have little interest in Christianity.

created the heavens and the earth." Arguably, that is the most important verse in the Bible. If God did not create all that exists, then you are of all persons most miserable since reading this booklet is, by definition, the most inordinate waste of time in which you could indulge. However, if the verse is accurate, then it follows that the world belongs to God, and His purposes in creation cannot be abridged without generating unhappiness and frustration in relation to both our Creator and His creation. Failure to discern the purpose and follow the intention of the Creator is construed as moral failure.

B.F. Skinner rejected this hypothesis, and many psychologists follow him in this disavowal. He says:

> Almost everyone makes ethical and moral judgments but this does not mean that the human species has "an inborn need or demand for ethical standards." [We could say as well that it has an inborn need or demand for unethical behavior, since almost everyone behaves unethically at some time or other.] Man has not evolved as an ethical or moral animal. He has evolved to the point at which he has constructed an ethical or moral culture. He differs from the other animals not in possessing a moral or ethical sense but

in having been able to generate a moral or ethical social environment.[5]

And Skinner is certainly correct. If there is no Creator, then there is no morality – only socially-agreed-upon convention, which will differ from one social order to the next.

In her scintillating monograph *Malpsychia*, Joyce Milton cites two examples of the destination of such thinking. She recounts the incident when Abe Maslow was speaking and openly espoused the abolition of churches and synagogues, replacing them with some sort of "religious surrogate." A largely Roman Catholic audience received him warmly with only one lonely nun asking penetrating questions. Of this experience, Maslow wrote, "They shouldn't applaud me—they should attack. If they were fully aware of what I was doing, they would."[6] Milton points here not only to Maslow's purpose but also to the credulity of the contemporary audience.

A second case cited by Milton is that of Carl Rogers, the father of Rogerian technique in counseling.

---

5 B.F. Skinner, *Beyond Freedom and Dignity* (New York: Bantam Books, 1971), 167. The sentence in brackets is part of Skinner's original work.

6 Joyce Milton, *The Road to Malpsychia: Humanistic Psychology and Our Discontents* (San Francisco: Encounter Books, 2002), 139.

Roger's wife, Helen, bore him two children and stood faithfully by him at every step. In her senior years she was ill and needed his assistance. Rogers complained in a public meeting that his wife's love for him had turned into a "clinging love," which he found objectionable. Explaining his dilemma, Milton alleges that Rogers said:

> If I give up my life or my personhood to take care of her, then I'm going to become bitter. I'm going to become angry inside at what I've given up. I'm not going to want to be with her—it would be out of a sense of duty—and that isn't the kind of relationship I want. It isn't the kind of relationship she would appreciate either, though she might think now that she would.[7]

These are the attitudes of those who accept neither the Creator nor His purpose in the earth. While there is much left to explain in human behavior, Freud taught his followers how to fog the atmosphere with pseudo-scientific jargon. Attempting to explain how conscience developed, Freud says in *Totem and Taboo*:

> Conscience is the internal perception of the rejection of a particular wish operating

---

7 Milton, *Road to Malpsychia,* 157.

within us. The stress, however, is upon the fact that this rejection has no need to appeal to anything else for support, that it is quite "certain of itself." This is even clearer in the case of consciousness of guilt—the perception of the internal condemnation of an act by which we have carried out a particular wish. To put forward any reason for this would seem superfluous: anyone who has a conscience must feel within him the justification for the condemnation, must feel the self-reproach for the act that has been carried out. This same characteristic is to be seen in the savage's attitude towards taboo. It is a command issued by conscience; and violation of it produces a fearful sense of guilt which follows as a matter of course and of which the origin is unknown.[8]

In stating this supposition he totally misses that the Greek word *suneideseis* actually means "know together with," implying that conscience is the product of the mind of man with the law of God or the presence of God or both.

---

8 Sigmund Freud, *Totem and Taboo*, translated by James Strachey (New York: W.W. Norton & Company, 1950), 68.

Accounting for the existence of morality or the presence of conscience provides some of the most difficult sledding for Darwinians. H. G. Wells claimed a bit too much when he suggested that Darwin destroyed the doctrine of the fall of man and unraveled the whole fabric of Christianity—without the fall there is no redemption and without redemption there is no Christianity.[9] But he was certainly correct in identifying the Darwinian intention.

The creation account of Genesis 1–3, if true, provides the following information. God created all that has existence (Col 1:17). In so doing, God had a purpose, and in that purpose humans—made in the *imago dei*—find meaning, significance, and happiness when and only when they are conformed to His will. Disastrously, men asserted their own wills in the place of God's will. This caused disruption of fellowship with God and is called sin. Not only did sin cause a breach in fellowship with God, but it is also the ultimate cause of the sufferings in human life. This lamentable state of affairs, however, can be countered by accepting and honoring these fundamental truths in the life of a believer.

A second fundamental truth is called regeneration. This occurs at the moment a man repents of his sin

---

9 Jerry Bergman, *The Darwin Effect: Its Influence on Nazism, Eugenics, Racism, Communism, Capitalism & Sexism* (Green Forest, AR: Master Books, 2014), 86.

and places faith in Christ. The Greek word *palingenesia* occurs only twice in the New Testament. The first occurrence in Matthew 19:28 references cosmic regeneration forecast for the *eschaton*. The second occurrence is in Titus 3:5 and refers to personal redemption. But the concept occurs with other terminology such as the discussion of the new birth in John 3. First Peter 1 speaks of the new birth, attributing this new state of affairs to the power of the resurrection of Christ. The word regeneration actually means "become again" and nullifies the effects of the Fall. Somehow God acts to create a new man. The regenerate man is not yet perfected. Shadows of his former life often darken his way a bit, but in the end he is still a new man. Something profound has happened to him, and he no longer sees with eyes of shame and guilt, but with the sober vision of forgiveness.

In his revealing book, *Unhinged*, psychiatrist Daniel Carlat puts on parade the series of events that led him to question the accepted path of psychiatry. He tells the story of David Foster Wallace, for example. This brilliant novelist with a cult-like following attempted every form of psychological cure available. One night, left at home by himself, he could stand it no longer; and he hung himself. Carlat, pensive in nature, saw too much. Reflecting on all of this, Carlat recognized that many carried problems that contemporary psychiatry could not help.[10] There remains a need for someone or something that can overcome the past and give new existence.

Allen Francis, chair of the DSM-4 Task Force, found himself in a similar dilemma and wrote in his monograph *Saving Normal*:

> Billions of research dollars have failed to produce convincing evidence that any mental disorder is a discrete disease entity with a unitary cause. Dozens of different candidate genes have been "found," but in follow-up studies each turned out to be fool's gold. Mental disorders are too heterogeneous in presentation and in causality to be considered simple diseases; instead each of our currently defined disorders will eventually turn out to be many different diseases. For now at least, Umpire One has been called out on strikes.[11]

---

10 Daniel J Carlat, *Unhinged: The Trouble with Psychiatry—A Doctor's Revelations about a Profession in Crisis* (New York: Free Press, 2010), 10.

11 Allen Frances, *Saving Normal: An Insider's Revolt Against Out-of-Control Psychiatric Diagnosis, DSM-5, Big Pharma, and the Medicalization of Ordinary Life* (New York: William Morrow, 2013), 19.

How could such a respected psychiatrist arrive at such a devastating conclusion? If he is right, then the need for a supernatural intervention called *the new birth* is the only answer.

A third fundamental truth concerns the New Testament instruction about the ministry of the Holy Spirit. Armed with a grasp of God's purpose in creation and protected by the regenerating prowess of the new birth, the Christian counselor may add to his arsenal the permanent and sanctioning indwelling of the Holy Spirit. First Corinthians 6:19 declares, "Or do you not know that your body is the temple of the Holy Spirit who is in you?" This remarkable affirmation is more startling than it appears on the surface. The word for temple is not *hieron* (Greek), referring to the whole temple complex, but *naos* (Greek), the Holy of Holies or the place where God dwells. That God through the Holy Spirit takes up a position in the body of the believer is most amazing. He becomes the captain of the soul and unleashes all the authority of the Godhead on behalf of a compliant believer. Freud saw these powers as meaningless and once again so did the vast majority of his offspring. In *Moses and Monotheism*, Freud notes that:

> Psychoanalytic research is in any case the subject of suspicious attention from Cathol-

icism. I do not maintain that this suspicion is unmerited. If our research leads us to a result that reduces religion to the status of a neurosis of mankind and explains its grandiose powers in the same way as we should a neurotic obsession in our individual patients, then we may be sure we shall incur in this country the greatest resentment of the powers that be.[12]

This indwelling of the Spirit means that while the psychiatrist and the pharmacologist must approach the counselee from the outside, attempting to penetrate the mysteries of the neuro-psychological system with theories that are often wrong and of little certainty, the Holy Spirit works from within knowing both the mind of the believer and the mind of God. From this position, He is able to produce the fruit of the Spirit: love, joy, peace, longsuffering, gentleness, kindness, goodness, faithfulness, and self-control, all of which drug-wielding psychiatrists only long to accomplish.

Admittedly, if the counselee is not a believer, then this ultimate weapon is not available as a resource. Even in this case, however, the Holy Spirit is actively convicting of sin, of righteousness, and of judgment

---

12 Sigmund Freud, *Moses and Monotheism*, translated by Katherine Jones (New York: Vintage Books, 1939), 68.

(John 16:8). The one seeking aid may not be regenerate, but he still has the witness of creation and the convicting ministry of the Holy Spirit. A wise counselor, being cognizant of this, will first build on the work of the Spirit toward the evangelization of the counselee.

A fourth fundamental truth focuses on the Bible itself. God has graciously provided one final formidable weapon to guide both counselor and counselee. God has revealed the mind of the Lord in the sacred text that we call the Bible. Biblical counselors know infinitely more about this ministry than a wandering theologian. But may I stir up your pure minds by reminding you of the extent and value of knowing and using the Bible? Moses has just extended the baton to Joshua who has already been running for a while. Yet God speaks now urging three times that Joshua be strong and of good courage. Specifically, Joshua is to be strong in that he is to observe all of the Law, which Moses delivered. He is not to allow the Law of God to depart from his mouth. He is to meditate on this Law and observe to do it (Josh 1:5-9). He must observe the law, meditate on the law, and keep the law close. Can you imagine a better description of a biblical counselor?

All Scripture is God-exhaled and is therefore profitable for doctrine, for reproof, for correction, and for instruction in righteousness. Through Scripture, the man of God is equipped for all good works (2 Tim 3:16-17). We are to desire it like new-born babes desire milk so that we may experience spiritual growth (1 Pet 2:2). But, someone will object, noting that there are many things the Bible does not address. There is no word about the profitability of the Word for the sport of bull riding; but there is a fair amount about wisdom, which might suggest staying off the bull altogether. In any event, the Word of God prepares you for everything.

The wisdom of Proverbs provides counsel on most areas of life. Job's friends provide counsel to him that is true more often than not. But because their counsel is offered with wrong motives and misapplication to Job, it is useless or harmful. Often conceived as a book that only helps with Job's particular dilemma, this important aspect of counseling requiring discernment and proper motivation is an added value in Job.

If I may be permitted a personal reflection and confession—as a youth, I had a problem with anger. I still have a problem with anger. What changed radically in my own life as a result of the reading of God's Word was my understanding of that anger. What I initially interpreted as righteous indignation, I have come to understand as *chutzpah* and pride. What I needed was Hermes to right my interpretation. But I had something better. Through the teaching ministry of the Holy Spirit within, augmented by verses including, "The wrath of man does not work the righteousness of God" (Jms 1:20) and "Wherefore let every man be swift to hear, slow to speak and slow to anger" (Jms 1:19), I was able to determine that anger was just my favorite form of sin and was the reason for my unhappiness. Stories of biblical characters like Joseph and Ruth taught me to trust the providence of God rather than my own unfiltered responses. Doubtless I will struggle with this all my life, but I will never again suggest even to myself that God is pleased with or ambivalent to this behavior. And as I overcome and trust Him alone for justice and mercy, life's quality and fulfillment increase exponentially.

Gary Greenberg, a Connecticut psychotherapist penned a volume called *The Book of Woe.* The subtitle is *The DSM and the UNMAKING of Psychiatry.* Like many others, Greenberg dissembled the DSM.[13] After 2000 years of efforts to do the same for the Bible, the Word of God stands triumphant over its enemies.

Calling the Church to Be the Church

My purpose here has not been to deliver a definitive judgment against the psychotherapeutic industry. As is

---

13 Gary Greenberg, *The Book of Woe: The DSM and the Unmaking of Psychiatry* (New York: Blue Rider Press, 2013), 13.

evident, I do believe America and much of the world have bought into a legend and paid a great amount of money for its purchase. But I leave the adjudication of that to God, who alone can judge such things. Rather, my purpose is to call the church to do what it alone can do.

We in the church cannot dispense drugs. We do not have the competence to make decisions in the world of neuroscience. But we do have the Word of God, and we know from experience that whenever people follow its dictates, they live happy and meaningful lives and handle stress with great emotional and mental dexterity. If there are exceptions to that, they are so infrequent that they should not interdict biblical counseling. Therefore, I conclude with this challenge to our churches and to our schools. Read Freud, Skinner, and all of their followers as philosophy and not as science—interesting but hardly determinative. Attempt finding all the answers to human problems in God's Word, for Jesus Christ is the Word. Teach the attitudes of the heart that change a man. Honor God in all things. This is our contribution to the beginning of revival in the churches.

On October 31, we frequently celebrate the posting of Martin Luther's *95 theses* and consequently the beginning of the Reformation. Recently, an increasing number of scholars have become aware of the amazing presence of a Reformation people who suffered profoundly—the Anabaptists. These Christians not only embraced *sola scriptura*, but they also lived by the Bible. Listen to the praise rendered to them by their enemies:

> Among the existing heretical sects there is none which in appearance leads a more modest or pious life than the Anabaptist[s]. As concerns their outward public life they are irreproachable. No lying, deception, swearing, strife, harsh language, no intemperate eating and drinking, no outward personal display, is found among them, but humility, patience, uprightness, neatness, honesty, temperance, straightforwardness in such measure that one would suppose that they had the Holy Spirit of God. (Franz Agricola)
>
> I frankly confess that in most [Anabaptists] there is in evidence piety and consecration and indeed a zeal which is beyond any suspicion of insincerity. For what earthly advantage could they hope to win by enduring exile, torture, and unspeakable punishment of the flesh? I testify before God that I cannot say that on account of a lack of

wisdom they are somewhat indifferent toward earthly things, but rather from divine
motives. (Capito) [14]

Hear Savonarola, a precursor to the Reformation,
moments before he was hung and consigned to the
flames:

Bring it on, the excommunication, bring
it in on a spear. I know that there are
those in Rome who are toiling against me
night and day, but O Lord, this is what I
desire. I crave only your cross, make me
to be persecuted. I ask you this grace;
that you do not let me die in my bed. [15]

And at the moment of death:

"I separate thee," pronounced the turncoat
bishop, "from the church militant and triumphant!"
Unable to keep silent, Savonarola replied, "Militant, not triumphant, for you

---

14 Harold S. Bender, *The Anabaptist Vision* (Scottsdale,
Pennsylvania: Herald Press, 1944), 23-24.
15 Douglas Bond and Douglas McComas, *Girolamo Savonarola* (Faverdale North, Darlington: E.P. Books, 2014), 105.

have no power to separate me from the church triumphant to which I go."

With a final sneer, the hangman checked the noose and gave a mighty heave. Savonarola fell. The noose did its work. He died instantly.[16]

Listen to Jakob Hutter as he faces his demise:

The priests, in their evil, vindictive passion, thought they would try to drive the devil out of him. So they had him dipped in ice-cold water and then taken into a hot room, where he was beaten with rods. They lacerated his body, poured brandy into the wounds, then set fire to it and let it burn. They tied his hands and feet and gagged him again so that he could not denounce their wickedness. Then they put a plumed hat on his head and took him into the house of their idols, because they knew how much he detested it. So they mocked and ridiculed him in every way they could think of.

A heroic fighter for Christ, he was unwavering in his faith. Therefore he was sentenced to death. After suffering much at

16 Bond and McComas, *Girolamo Savonarola*, 135.

the hands of evil men, the brood of Caiaphas and Pilate, he was burned alive at the stake.

As he was being led to the fire he said, "Now come here, all you disputers, and let us prove our faith in the fire. This fire will not harm my soul any more than the fiery furnace harmed Shadrach, Meshach, and Abednego."[17]

Those who ostensibly had desperate need of Freud and Skinner found Jesus and the Bible totally satisfactory in the hour of greatest need. May we do the same.

---

17 Jakob Hutter, *Brotherly Faithfulness: Epistles from a Time of Persecution* (Rifton, NY: Plough Publishing House, 1979), 202.

CHAPTER 2

---·-⟨∞⟩-·---

Biblical Counseling
and the Church

More than eighteen hundred years of the history of Christianity passed before the study of psychology as a discipline was introduced to society. Lost people suffered serious problems, and the saints frequently encountered similar difficulties. Spiritual conflict was unavoidable then as now. And the churches responded not only with treatises about the nature of man but also with intense pastoral care. Much of this was accomplished through the teaching ministry of the church; but even if normally hidden from public view, pastors doubtless spent untold hours with both saints and sinners doing what is today termed "counseling."

THE GENESIS OF CONTEMPORARY PSYCHOLOGY

In 1890, Sigmund Freud began a distinguished career of publishing, which launched the discipline of psychology into popular acceptance. Wilhelm Wundt, a German physician, developed a laboratory for psychological research at the University of Leipzig in 1879. This date is regarded by many as the birth date of modern psychology and Wundt as the father of psychology. But efforts of understanding and interpreting human behavior, even including hospitals for psychologically troubled patients, are found in medieval Moslem society and in even more ancient societies. But with the work of Sigmund Freud and of William James, the first to teach psychology in an American university, modern psychology arrived on the radar of the world.

From that launch of psychology at the University of Vienna, a vast program of psychological and psychiatric endeavors, which blossomed into a multi-billion dollar industry, developed. Pharmaceuticals have profited exponentially from the development of medications employed in psychiatric medicine. The system of jurisprudence in America has introduced practitioners of these "arts" into the legal system where they often serve as "experts" influencing renderings of both judge and jury. In time, the influence of psychology, psycho-therapy, and psychiatric medicine became so prevalent as to maintain unquestioned acquiescence and unchallenged hegemony.

For the purposes of this assessment, psychiatric medicine is beyond the scope of consideration. This is not to give psychiatry a clean bill, but the use of "talk therapy" is the immediate concern of churches and church-related institutions. Present programs do not include medical training but rather the processes and procedures of psychological "talk therapy." Increasingly these efforts employ the jargon of the psychiatric at the expense of exclusion or diminution of biblical principles.

Concerns about the runaway train called psychology are not the sole property of Bible-thumpers or unsophisticated evangelicals. Increasingly these concerns arise among psychologists themselves. In *Manufacturing Victims*, subtitled *What the Psychology Industry is Doing to People*, psychologist Tana Dineen laments the deleterious effects within the social order from making *victims* rather than responsible citizens out of a large portion of the population of North America:

> Psychologizing assumes as its basis an interior world in which an Unconscious has profound influence and power, a place where

things are different from what they seem on the outside and can only be discovered, understood, explained, and changed with the help and direction of psychologists. And it relies on the belief that, like guides familiar with the terrain, psychologists can see what is hidden there: what is not known (about the past), what can't be seen (in the present), and what must be discovered (to achieve a better future).

Psychologizing involves:

1) constructing a theory about victimization,
2) applying that theory to individuals,
3) turning personal events into psychological symbols, which are expressed in psychological language,
4) creating the need for psychologists who can interpret the symbols.[18]

My own approach has been to speak of psychology as a "soft science," along with sociology and not a few other subjects of education. This is distinct from

---

18 Tana Dineen, *Manufacturing Victims: What the Psychology Industry is Doing to People*, 2nd ed. (Montreal: Robert Davies Multimedia Publishing,1998), 39.

the sciences, which as physics, for example, can actually demonstrate the truth of gravity or the laws of thermodynamics. But Dineen, citing Victor Raimy, is less generous:

> At the 1949 Boulder Conference on Graduate Education in Clinical Psychology, Victor Raimy is quoted as having said: "Psychotherapy is an undefined technique applied to unspecified cases with unpredictable results. For this technique, rigorous training is required." [72] 19

Or again:

> What is now called "psychology" is, to use Huber's term, "junk science" rooted in neither, with no soul or science, no boundaries and no method; swept along by the shifting ground of popular belief and the ephemeral demands for expert opinion. There is little, if any, similarity between this pseudoscience

---

19 Dineen, *Manufacturing Victims*, 123. The information in footnote 72, which is included in the quote above, is found on p. 136 in Dineen's volume and comes from Perry London and Gerald L. Klerman, "Evaluating Psychotherapy," *American Journal of Psychiatry*, 139:6, June 1982, p. 709.

and the real science on which traditional psychology was founded.[20]

Dineen's concluding assessment of the impact of psychology is less than flattering:

> At the beginning of this century, the discipline of psychology held all the hopes, aspirations and promise of a new-born science. Now, at the end of the century, it is evident that psychology has failed to live up to these. Rather, it epitomizes the self-serving, boastful nature of an adolescent; an entrepreneurial pseudoscience. Despite its popularity, it has not produced the society, free of crime and problems, that it had claimed it would. Psychology has neither provided a better understanding of the psyche, nor created a healthier way of living. In fact, as the number of psychologists has increased in the past three decades so has crime, poverty, homelessness and anxiety increased; in other words, "the world is getting worse."[132] It is clear that the Psychology Industry, put to the test, has failed to prove itself.[21]

---

20 Dineen, *Manufacturing Victims*, 140.
21 Ibid., 175. The information in footnote 132, which

If Dineen is alarmed about the psychology industry and the producing of victims, Kirk, Gomory, and
Cohen chronicle the extent of the problem:

> Over the last fifty years in the United
> States, there has been a massive expansion
> of the psychiatric enterprise. According
> to one source (Frank & Glied, 2006), the
> principal group of mental health profes-
> sionals in 1950 used to be made up of about
> seven thousand psychiatrists. Today, using
> the US Department of Labor (2012) figures
> and selecting professions with the terms
> *psychiatric, mental health, substance abuse,*
> as well as *clinical psychologists* and *mental
> health* and *substance abuse social workers*, we
> have an army of at least six hundred thou-
> sand mental health professionals. By adding
> psychiatric nurses and a number of other
> counseling and therapeutic occupations
> and their supporting staff, such as medical
> records keepers and various mental health
> technicians, the number would easily top

is included in the quote above, is found on page 197 in Dineen's
volume: "Hillman, James and Ventura, Michael. *We've had a Hundred Years of Psychotherapy and the World is Getting Worse.* San
Francisco: HarperCollins, 1992."

one million. Not surprisingly, the amount spent on what are called mental health services has also exploded, from about $1 billion in 1956 (Frank & Glied, 2006) to $113 billion today (Garfield, 2011).[22]

With wide acceptance of the nomenclature of the psychological industry, to say nothing of the genuflection of the church to the priesthood of therapists, there have been some who have consistently resisted the notion that the emperor's wardrobe was something more than severely limited. But they are in the minority. Indeed, the churches, for various reasons, seem to have ceded the care of souls to the psychological enterprise. Even though many of those congregations employ their own counselors instead of referring counselees to secular counseling services, often

---

22 Stuart A. Kirk, Tomi Gomory, & David Cohen, *Mad Science: Psychiatric Coercion, Diagnosis, and Drugs* (New Brunswick: Transaction Publishers, 2013), vii. Within this quote, the authors cite three additional resources and note them on page xii of their work: "Frank, R.G., & Glied, S.A. (2006). *Better but not well: Mental health policy in the United States since 1950.* Baltimore: Johns Hopkins University Press. Garfield, R.L. (2011). *Mental health financing in the United States: A primer.* Washington, DC: Kaiser Commission on Medicaid and the Uninsured. US Department of Labor (2012). Occupational employment and wages—May 2011. Bureau of Labor Statistics. Retrieved from: http://www.bls.gov/news.release/archives/ocwage_03272012.pdf."

those employed by churches are already steeped in the jargon and, more than they recognize, in the practices of secular psychotherapy. Even when baptized with Christian concepts and verbiage, the therapy offered seldom arises from the counsel of God enshrined in the Scriptures.

In the secular world, this psychologizing proceeds almost along religious lines, in this classic passage Milton observes:

> It is just possible that a randomly selected group of Americans could sit down over coffee at their neighborhood diner and come up with a reasonable secularized translation of the Ten Commandments—though, of course, the Diner Decalogue wouldn't have quite the same ring of authority. In real life, however, such tasks have tended to be assigned to experts like the faculty of the Harvard Graduate School of Education. And experience has shown that they couldn't do the job, even if they wanted to. Obviously, the HGSE people would begin by throwing out commandments one through three, since they assume the existence of a single deity and are offensive to atheists and Wiccans. The injunction to honor one's father and mother

would need to be reworked, since rebellion against the patriarchy is a virtue. "Thou shalt not steal" would be out, since expropriating property may not be wrong under all circumstances, especially for members of exploited groups. Adultery, of course, is purely a private matter. And as for coveting . . . who really cares? "Thou shalt not kill" would probably make the cut, though it would likely be reduced to a condemnation of capital punishment.[23]

None of this should actually be astonishing to thinking Christians. The overwhelming majority of the advocates of psychotherapy have not been from the ranks of evangelical Christians. Indeed many like Sigmund Freud and B. F. Skinner were atheists. Abetted since 1859 by Darwinism's reduction of humans to the status of highly evolved animals and encouraging doctrines like "the survival of the fittest," Skinner's conclusion that humans have neither freedom nor dignity is hardly surprising. As Skinner, the behaviorist declaims:

23 Joyce Milton, *The Road to Malpsychia: Humanistic Psychology and Our Discontents* (San Francisco: Encounter Books, 2002), 265.

What is being abolished is autonomous man—the inner man, the homunculus, the possessing demon, the man defended by the literatures of freedom and dignity.

His abolition has long been overdue. Autonomous man is a device used to explain what we cannot explain in any other way. He has been constructed from our ignorance, and as our understanding increases, the very stuff of which he is composed vanishes. Science does not dehumanize man, it de-homunculizes him, and it must do so if it is to prevent the abolition of the human species. To man *qua* man we readily say good riddance. Only by dispossessing him can we turn to the real causes of human behavior. Only then can we turn from the inferred to the observed, from the miraculous to the natural, from the inaccessible to the manipulable.[24]

One may be forgiven for inquiry as to why these atheistic origins of psychotherapy are not recognized, read, taught, and thoroughly and biblically critiqued. Listen to Skinner's theory:

---

24 B. F. Skinner, *Beyond Freedom & Dignity* (New York: Bantam/Vintage Books, 1971), 191.

The concept of a responsibility offers little help. The issue is controllability. We cannot change genetic defects by punishment; we can work only through genetic measures which operate on a much longer time scale. What must be changed is not the responsibility of autonomous man but the conditions, environmental or genetic, of which a person's behavior is a function.[25]

Why not determine what Freud thought about God, anthropology, law, the Jews, etc.? Why not read *Moses and Monotheism* and *Totem and Taboo*?[26] Why not demonstrate for students the simple truth stated by Jesus when He poignantly observed:

Even so, every good tree bears good fruit, but a bad tree bears bad fruit. A good tree cannot bear bad fruit nor *can* a bad tree bear good fruit. Every tree that does not bear good fruit is cut down and thrown into the

---

25 Skinner, *Beyond Freedom & Dignity*, 71.

26 Sigmund Freud, *Moses and Monotheism*, trans. Katherine Jones (New York: Vintage Books, 1939); idem, *Totem and Taboo: Some Points of Agreement between the Mental Lives of Savages and Neurotics*, trans. James Strachey (New York: W. W. Norton & Company, Inc., 1950).

fire. Therefore by their fruits you will know them (Matt 7:17–20).

PSYCHOLOGY RESPONDS

A common response from those who desire a more integrated approach to the counseling curriculum proceeds along two lines. First, we do not teach Sigmund Freud, Carl Jung, Victor Franckl, Abraham Maslow, etc. anymore. These progenitors of psychotherapy have long since been abandoned. Second, even secularists working in clinical environments have the opportunity to observe human behavior and draw helpful conclusions, which, in turn, may prove helpful to Christian therapists. One must candidly reply that there is some truth in both. But in *Malpsychia*, as Milton notes concerning some failed self-esteem study groups:

> However, as the article makes clear, that doesn't mean that Furlong has changed his mind in any fundamental way. His prediction that the same ideas will be repackaged under a different label recalls Carl Rogers' comment that it will be necessary to keep changing the name of the encounter group

movement to keep one step ahead of the critics.[27]

And that is exactly part of the problem. The sciences are subject to revision upon new discovery. But no science has so frequently changed its positions as has psychology in its 120-year history. As Milton regrets that this is made necessary to stay one step ahead of the critics. But there is more. While the target keeps moving and while new syndromes and neuroses arise with alarming regularity, these do not constitute new sources but rather new streams flowing into the winding river of erroneous assumptions laid down by the secularists. In 2010 *World* published an article about the next edition of the *Diagnostic and Statistical Manual of Mental Disorders*, the bible of psychotherapy, affectionately known as the DSM-IV.[28] Jerome C. Wakefield, a New York psychiatrist, is cited as having concerns about over-diagnosis:

---

27 Milton, *Malpsychia*, 263-64, referring to the quotation of Michael Furlong, "a professor from the University of California at Santa Barbara who is engaged in training school psychologists," in "a 1999 *Los Angeles Times* article headlined 'Losing Faith in Self-Esteem.'" Milton says, "Furlong agrees that self-esteem has been so debunked that 'the only people who use [the term] are those who want to discredit the idea'" (263).

28 *Diagnostic and Statistical Manual of Mental Disorders*, 4th ed. text revision: DSM-IV®-TR (Washington, DC: American Psychiatric Association, 2000). Now the DSM-V is available.

The psychosis risk syndrome is a bad precedent. A lot of things give you risk for disorder. I mean, running for a bus increases your probability of a heart attack temporarily and so on. You could start pathologizing everything in life if you start pathologizing risk.[29]

The DSM is essential to the psychotherapist if he wishes medical insurance to pay for counseling sessions. The 10"x7"x2¼" tome must be used by the therapist to identify the client's malady. These include amazing categories such as Body Dysmorphic Disorder, a preoccupation with a defect in appearance real or imagined.[30] Or how about Paraphilias, which is characterized as "recurrent, intense sexual urges, fantasies, or behaviors that involve unusual objects, activities, or situations and cause clinically significant distress or impairment in social, occupational, or other important areas of functioning."[31]

Please forgive the intrusion of theology at this point; but where I come from, that is called lasciviousness, lust, lawlessness, trespass, transgression, ungodli-

---

29 Quoted by Daniel James Devine in "Hoarders Beware," *World* 10 April 2010, 56.

30 DSM-IV®-TR, 507-10.

31 Ibid., 535.

ness, lewdness, dissipation, disobedience or, in a pinch, just plain sin. Where do these kinds of conclusions originate? Even if much of the methodology of Freud has been abandoned, the DSM is thoroughly grounded in the atheism, secularism, and Darwinism of the early psychological thinking. The DSM is employed in any school that plans to graduate counselors who intend to be licensed. Even if critiqued, the absurdities of this monograph play an important role in the state's expectation in licensure. And make no mistake; this volume is not the friend of Christianity or of the Holy Scriptures.

But the DSM is hardly alone. Consider the American Counseling Association's *Ethical Standards Casebook*, which is utilized in most schools with a licensure-track curriculum:

> Two very different but complementary ways of reasoning about ethics are principle ethics and virtue ethics. **Principle ethics** traditionally has been espoused in the fields of medicine and bioethics (Cottone & Tarvydas, 2003) as well as by the counseling profession. In this approach, certain moral principles—or generally accepted assumptions or values in society—are seen as

fundamental to ethical reasoning. They are viewed as *prima facie* binding; that is, they must always be considered when counselors work to resolve an ethical dilemma. The following five moral principles generally are seen as being essential to counseling practice.

Autonomy refers to independence and self-determination. Under this principle, counselors respect the freedom of clients to choose their own directions, make their own choices, and control their own lives. We have an ethical obligation to decrease client dependency and foster independent decision making. We refrain from imposing goals, avoid being judgmental, and are accepting of different values.[32]

This is directly contradictory to the prophetic nature of the Scriptures. Yet a licensure track pressures counselors, either openly or surreptitiously, to withhold biblical morality. Consider this further assessment from the manual:

---

32 Barbara Herlihy and Gerald Corey, *ACA Ethical Standards Casebook*, 6th ed. (Alexandria, VA: American Counseling Association, 2006), 9.

Counselors are aware of their own values, attitudes, beliefs, and behaviors and avoid imposing values that are inconsistent with counseling goals. Counselors respect the diversity of clients, trainees, and research participants.

Katy, a school counselor, has strong personal beliefs against abortion. Mandy, a 15-year-old girl, comes to see the counselor because she is pregnant and wants information about the physical and emotional effects of an abortion. Katy responds with factual information about the emotional effects and suggests that Mandy talk with the school nurse about physical effects. Katy asks Mandy whether she has discussed this decision with her parents. Mandy asks if she can bring her parents in to talk about the situation in the counselor's presence. Katy agrees to the request. Throughout the family session, Katy remains objective and does not try to promote her antiabortion beliefs.[33]

To what have our churches come? Sin is not wrong merely because God decrees it to be so but also because of its destruction to meaningful life, hap-

---

33 Herlihy and Corey, *ACA Ethical Standards Casebook*, 63.

piness, right relationship to God and to neighbor, and ultimately to life and eternity! Sin is so unbelievably destructive that the Second Person of the triune God became incarnate to save men from what—a syndrome that they could not avoid and for which they carried no guilt?

Still another text employed in most licensure programs gives a typical assessment for counselors working with homosexuals:

Hermann and Herlihy (2006) summarize some of the legal aspects of the *Bruff* case:[34]

---

34 Gerald Corey, Marianne Schneider Corey, and Patrick Callanan, *Issues and Ethics in the Helping Professions*, 8th ed. (Belmont, CA: Brooks/Cole, Cengage Learning, 2011,2007), 138-41, a section on "A Court Case Involving a Therapist's Refusal to Counsel Homosexual Clients," explaining that Hermann and Herlihy, in their article, "Legal and Ethical Issues in Counseling Homosexual Clients," cite *Bruff v. North Mississippi Health Services, Inc.* (2001). Corey, Corey, and Callanan explain: "In 1996 Jane Doe initiated a counseling relationship with Bruff, a counselor employed at the North Mississippi Medical Center, an employee assistance program provider. After several sessions, Jane Doe informed Bruff that she was a lesbian and wanted to explore her relationship with her partner. Bruff refused on the basis of her religious beliefs, but offered to counsel her in other areas. The client (Jane Doe) discontinued counseling, and her employer filed a complaint with Bruff's agency . . . . Eventually, Bruff was dismissed by her employer" (138).

- The court held that the employer did make reasonable attempts to accommodate Bruff's religious beliefs.
- Bruff's inflexibility and unwillingness to work with anyone who has conflicting beliefs is not protected by the law.
- A counselor who refuses to work with homosexual clients can cause harm to them. The refusal to work on a homosexual client's relationship issues constitutes illegal discrimination.
- Counselors cannot use their religious beliefs to justify discrimination based on sexual orientation, and employers can terminate counselors who engage in this discrimination.

Hermann and Herlihy believe the *Bruff* case sets an important legal precedent. They assert that the appeals court decision is consistent with the Supreme court's precedent interpreting employers' obligations to make reasonable accommodations for employees' religious beliefs. From a legal perspective, the court case clarifies that refusing to counsel homosexual clients on relationship matters can result in the loss of a therapist's job. A homosexual client who sues a counselor for refusing to work with the client on issues related to sexual orientation is also likely to prevail in a malpractice suit as the counselor could be found in violation of the standard of care in the community. Hermann and Herlihy also note that the *Bruff* case raises an ethical issue that counselors often struggle with: When is it appropriate, and on what grounds, to refer a client?[35]

To make clear what is being stated, in the event that a practicing homosexual approaches a state-licensed counselor seeking the counselor's assistance in developing a more satisfactory relationship with his homosexual partner, not only can that counselor not tell him that his behavior is wrong and destructive, but also the counselor cannot recuse himself for religious reasons. The latter case, of course, is a violation of the counselor's First Amendment rights; but make no mistake: Licensed counselors carry the increasing burden, which churchmen, at least to date, do not face.

---

35 Corey, Corey, and Callanan, *Issues and Ethics.*, 139.

But shouldn't one read such psychological books? As a theologian, I read Bultmann, Barth, Schleiermacher, *The Shack*, *Blue Like Jazz*, etc., ad infinitum. And I have my student pastors read them. However, the following regimen is faithfully followed. First, I would never recommend these books to the congregants whom these pastors will serve. Two, I vigorously critique erroneous and suspect conclusions and faulty reasoning for the students who are reading such materials. I follow this protocol not only from common sense and logic but also because I thoroughly understand the Bible. Third, I then provide, from the Scriptures and from a decisively Christian worldview, an extensive evangelical alternative and strongly advocate that view. Anything less than this commitment is unworthy of a Christian institution, which is useless if the Christian perspective is not paramount in everything that is said or done?

What is to be learned from secular psychology? Doesn't the observation of human behavior in many clinical situations count for something? Clinical pathologists do not see much that a pastor does not encounter over a ten-year time span. However, I am prepared to grant that knowledge is helpful wherever it is found. Reading case histories from clinical efforts may well prove helpful to the counselor. But, even then, none is presented without presuppositions and spin, and the Christian counselor must read critically as well as from a biblical perspective. However, he can do this evaluation without the necessity of gullibility.

A LEGITIMATE QUESTION

The church of the Lord Jesus has three principal assignments. First, the saving gospel of Christ is to be taken to the ends of the earth. Second, those who receive the gospel and place their trust in Christ are to be baptized according to Christ's command. Finally, the teaching ministry of the church is to instruct these new believers in "all things that Jesus commanded" (Matt 28:16-20). There is a sense in which counseling may be a significant factor in all three assignments. Though people come to faith in Christ through a variety of means, one of the most frequent paths is through personal witness. An individual sharing his faith with one who is unregenerate is the most crucial form of counseling—one for which there cannot be too much preparation or passion. The counseling of baptismal candidates also requires skill and understanding; but, tragically this instruction is almost totally neglected. Any school of counseling in an institution purporting to follow Christ ought to devote special attention to these two mandates of the Great Commission.

However, the third part of the commission, "teaching them to observe all things that I have commanded," entails much of the counseling effort. "Teaching" also happens in varied venues. The pastor's consistent exposition and application of the text of Scripture and the teaching ministry of the whole church are not only invaluable but also offer sufficient instructions in life and faith for all. However, individuals still often face serious problems, either internally or relationally, which merit the wisdom of a seasoned, thoroughly biblically-literate man or woman of faith, who, exercising the gift of patience, can listen empathetically to the difficulties of others, explain the wisdom of the Scriptures to them, and assist them in developing ways to begin to apply this wisdom to their own disturbing situations.

A Christian counselor, in contradistinction to a counselor who is a Christian, enjoys an advantage at this point. First, he knows well the problems associated with human inability or what theologians call "depravity." Succinctly stated, "The natural man does not receive the things of the Spirit of God, for they are foolishness to him; nor can he know them, because they are spiritually discerned" (1 Cor 2:14). Hence, all "talk therapy" operates with severe limitations. While the counselor may provide accurate assessment and biblical direction, the natural man has neither the ability to comprehend this counsel nor the dynamic to pursue it thoroughly. However, the Christian counselor, unhindered by ecclesiastical or political regulations can press the counselee to seek the only solution that is ultimately curative and satisfactory. Any commitment of a Christian entity that prohibits such a witness under the guise of "imposing one's own beliefs on another" is in violation of the task assigned by Jesus and must be emphatically rejected by Christian counselors.

Once a "client" has experienced "godly sorrow that leads to repentance" (2 Cor 7:10) and the one seeking assistance has trusted in Jesus for salvation, the counseling prospects become brighter still. Now the counselor is assisting someone who is a new person (2 Cor 5:17), who has been "born again" (John 3:5), and who is, therefore, regenerated or made new (Titus 3:5) and who is no longer a "natural man" (1 Cor 2:14). He may yet be an infant or a "carnal man" (1 Cor 2:15-16), but he is a new man. The old man has died, and a new man lives (Rom 8:1-17). He now has the ability to grasp the wisdom of God and the impetus to do so.

The wisdom of God is available to this new man in Holy Scripture. God acted in history to reveal all that people need to know in order to be right with God, right with others, and right with oneself, "For the grace of God that brings salvation has appeared to all men, teaching us that, denying ungodliness and worldly lusts, we should live soberly, righteously, and godly in the present age" (Titus 2:11-12). Nowhere in special revelation does God directly address mainlining heroin or sexting on iPhones. But the basis for those behaviors and all other destructive human behavior is clearly identified in Scripture, together with God's remedy.

A new, regenerated follower of Christ now has before him the perfect instruction of Christ in the Bible. He can read the instruction. The counselor can point the counselee to these words of divine wisdom. Thus a Christian counselor should have the same grasp of his Bible as the pastor! But how can the counselee find the impetus to do what he reads in Scripture? In the graciousness of God, this new man with God's manual of instruction for life has also become the "temple of God." He has been permanently indwelt by the Holy Spirit. The indwelling Spirit of God operates on numerous levels in the life of the believer. He teaches the word (1 John 2:27), provides escape from evil (1 Cor 10:13), continually renews the new man (Titus 3:5), magnifies Christ (John 16:14), produces the fruit of the Spirit (Gal 5:22-23), and so on.

Now add the overwhelming confidence of this new man in Christ, indwelt by the Spirit and armed with Scripture in the all-pervading providence of a gracious, loving, just, and righteous God; and everything needed by the Christian counselor is available.

Never have I been bothered that the secular psychological industry recognizes none of this and insists that more is needed. **What does seem stunning is that many churches and believers do not comprehend it, or even support it!** In possession of a spiritual gold mine, many believers shuffle off in search of the copper pennies of a failed world. Esau still markets his birthright for a mess of pottage.

Consequently, for some years I have been asking a question addressed to Christians in the psychotherapeutic industry. If a person has been saved, born again, regenerated, and has been indwelt by God Himself in the person of the Holy Spirit and if he has the Bible–God's Word about how to live and die, and if he is aware of the providences of God, exactly what more does he need? I have received no poor answers from Christians in psychotherapy. I have received no answers at all! Until I receive adequate and convincing answers concerning the inadequacy of these four spiritual truths, I will continue to insist that the quest for spiritual, mental, and emotional health is the task of the church and the church alone. Neither our pulpits nor our counseling rooms have need of government sanction.[36] To seek or accept such control is unacceptable and a compromise.

---

36 As indicated earlier, the practice of psychiatric medicine, the use of calming drugs, and even the incarceration of those deemed dangerous to themselves or others is not a consideration in this book. Understanding and charting the functions of the brain and the effect of medication is legitimate science. Even here, however, the Christian must be cautioned that demonstrable evidence of many of the theories associated with that practice is in short supply. For a fascinating look at the essential failures of such endeavors see Michel Foucault, *Madness and Civilization: A History of Insanity in the Age of Reason*, trans. Richard Howard (New York: Vintage Books, 1965), and Simon Winchester, *The Professor and the Madman: A Tale of Murder, Insanity, and the Making of the* Oxford English Dictionary (New York: HarperCollins, 1998). The former chronicles the abandonment of community responsibility and the move to incarceration while the latter tells the absorbing story of a major contributor to the *Oxford English Dictionary*.

CHAPTER 3

————⟨∞⟩————

The Sufficiency
of the Scriptures

Suppose that you are at peace with God, at peace with others, and at peace with yourself. Suppose further that you are confident of God's goodness, justice, knowledge of all things, and ability to manage all things. Imagine that you believe that God has spoken clearly in both mandates and principles and that through a breathtaking experience of regeneration your impulses toward God have been awakened and your inclination toward rebellion has been dealt a mortal wound. And finally, imagine that somehow God has taken up residence in your body as a permanent pilot and prompter from within.

Enshrined in these suppositions are the doctrines of theology, anthropology, soteriology, revelation, and providence. Armed with such a panoply, it is difficult to imagine precisely what is missing from the believer's arsenal. What exactly can the soft sciences deliver that is not already available in a proper relationship to God and a commitment to His instruction in the Bible?

Please do not hear this as a conclusion that nothing can be learned from the soft sciences. Neither should this be dismissed as more fundamentalist diatribe and obscurantism. Quite to the contrary, my own dissatisfaction with some versions of nouthetic counseling, especially in the academy, is its inadequate tendency to acquaint students with the history and conclusions of the soft sciences. One need not overly imbibe, for example, in Christian critiques of "psychobabble." Unbelievers have written far more compelling critiques of the psychological industry. Michael Alan Taylor in his thoughtful 2013 work cryptically entitled *Hippocrates Cried*, writes as an unbelieving but honest and observant psychiatrist concerning the current violations of the Hippocratic Oath:

> As we have learned more and more about the brain and how it generates complex behaviors, U.S. psychiatry remains wedded to a diagnostic and treatment system over 60 years old: identify a few clinical features that are said to work for that match a di-

agnostic label in the *DSM* and then apply the treatments that are said to work for that category of patient. It is cookbook diagnosis and treatment. Without thought, labels are applied and drugs with significant side effects but with only modest efficacy are prescribed. Various brands of psychotherapy are offered with little consideration of what actually helps and which patients are best suited to a particular brand. This is twenty-first-century U.S. psychiatry. As a field we have in my view ignored the oath to first, do no harm.[37]

Robert Whitaker concludes,

However, in this book, we have been focusing on the role that psychiatry and its medications may be playing in this epidemic, and the evidence is quite clear. First, by greatly expanding diagnostic boundaries, psychiatry is inviting an ever-greater number of children and adults into the mental illness camp. Second, those so diagnosed are then treated with psychiatric medications that

---

37 Michael Alan Taylor, *Hippocrates Cried: The Decline of American Psychiatry* (Oxford: Oxford University Press, 2013), 49.

increase the likelihood they will become chronically ill. Many treated with psychotropics end up with new and more severe psychiatric symptoms, physically unwell, and cognitively impaired. That is the tragic story writ large in five decades of scientific literature.[38]

Again, my purpose is not to denigrate psychology. My purpose is to point out that the enthusiastic and optimistic endorsement of the culture for contemporary psychotherapeutic methods neither is unanimous nor is its criticism the province of unlettered, squeamish theologians in library cubicles. If clergy and the church elect to follow the pastoral counseling techniques prescribed in the Bible, they are following an ancient and generally successful approach even as they confess that pharmacology and medicine are not their fields of experience or confidence. Neither are we saying that we are content to remain in ignorance.

My students are asked to read Sigmund Freud's *Totem and Taboo* (1913), *The Future of an Illusion* (1927), and *Moses and Monotheism* (1939). According to this last volume, Moses was actually an Egyptian who was

---

38 Robert Whitaker, *Anatomy of An Epidemic: Magic Bullets, Psychiatric Drugs, and the Astonishing Rise of Mental Illness in America* (New York: Broadway Books, 2010), 209.

somehow connected to Akhenaten, the monotheistic pharaoh of Egypt. He eventually led out a small group of followers who became disillusioned with Moses when he required them all to be circumcised. This led them to kill Moses resulting in corporate and individual guilt feelings, which drive the Jewish religion until today. The male students tend to identify with the reticence about adult circumcision but otherwise find the whole projected scenario ludicrous.

Then I insist that they read B.F. Skinner's *Beyond Freedom and Dignity* in which they discover that they are little more than automatons, void of any sort of actual freedom or dignity. Cap it off with a reading of Michael Foucault's *Madness and Civilization*. My son likes to say that "Foucault is Dad's favorite French philosopher, but he reads them all." Indeed, add my favorite liberal theologian, Harvey Cox, on *The Feast of Fools*, and you have a reading list, the consumption of which will convert many a thoughtful reader to the superiority of the Christian faith. Just listen to Skinner:

> Careless references to purpose are still to be found in both physics and biology, but good practice has no place for them; yet almost everyone attributes human behavior to intentions, purposes, aims, and goals. If it is still possible to ask whether a machine

can show purpose, the question implies, significantly, that if it can it will more closely resemble a man.[39]

Pastoral theology has a long and in many cases noble history. But, what did the church do before modern psychotherapy? Freud lived from 1856 to 1939. How did God's people navigate the rapids of life's river before that? At least I would suppose that mental and emotional triage was considerably less costly.

But my purpose is not to mount an assault on secular psychology. Let them help all that they can but be certain they bear responsibility for the results. And if hard science claims are made, hold them to the same standards of evidence that a biologist, chemist, or geneticist would be expected to maintain.

Rather, my interest is in the pastoral guidance provided for the churches. Here, to return to my suppositions, I believe that we can build an excellent case for the sufficiency of Scripture in providing adequate, even superlative, guidance for troubled saints. There are, I believe, four salient truths to be vigorously asserted as the essential backdrop for all pastoral counseling:

- the regenerating experience of the New Birth

---

39 B. F. Skinner, *Beyond Freedom & Dignity* (New York: Bantam/Vintage Books, 1971), 6.

- the permanent indwelling of God's Holy Spirit
- the Bible as a text providing the actions and attributes that God has promised to bless, and
- an understanding of the purposes of God in creation.

Here is some of the biblical direction.

I. **Revelation:** The act of God in which He imparts to humans made in His image the portion of His own mind that is essential for life and meaning, both temporal and eternal.

A. The Nature of Revelation

1. **Exodus 32:15–16** And Moses turned and went down from the mountain, and the two tablets of the Testimony were in his hand. The tablets were written on both sides; on the one side and on the other they were written. Now the tablets were the work of God, and the writing was the writing of God engraved on the tablets.

2. **Hosea 1:1–2** The word of the LORD that came to Hosea the son of Beeri, in the days of Uzziah, Jotham, Ahaz, and Hezekiah, kings of Judah, and in the days of Jeroboam the son of Joash, king of Israel. When the LORD began to speak by Hosea, the LORD said to Hosea:

"Go, take yourself a wife of harlotry and children of harlotry, for the land has committed great harlotry by departing from the LORD."

3. **2 Timothy 3:16** All Scripture is given by inspiration of God, and is profitable for doctrine, for reproof, for correction, for instruction in righteousness.

4. **2 Peter 1:16–21** For we did not follow cunningly devised fables when we made known to you the power and coming of our Lord Jesus Christ, but were eyewitnesses of His majesty. For He received from God the Father honor and glory when such a voice came to Him from the Excellent Glory: "This is My beloved Son, in whom I am well pleased." And we heard this voice which came from heaven when we were with Him on the holy mountain. And so we have the prophetic word confirmed, which you do well to heed as a light that shines in a dark place, until the day dawns and the morning star rises in your hearts; knowing this first, that no prophecy of Scripture is of any private interpretation, for prophecy never came by the will of man, but holy men of God spoke as they were moved by the Holy Spirit.

B. Comprehensive Principles: God does not directly address stem cell research, bacteriological or chemical warfare or even abortion or slavery.

1. **Matthew 22:34–40** But when the Pharisees heard that He had silenced the Sadducees, they gathered together. Then one of them, a lawyer, asked Him a question, testing Him, and saying, "Teacher, which is the great commandment in the law?" Jesus said to him, "You shall love the LORD your God with all your heart, with all your soul, and with all your mind. This is the first and great commandment. And the second is like it: You shall love your neighbor as yourself. On these two commandments hang all the Law and the Prophets."

2. **1 Corinthians 8:13** Therefore, if food makes my brother stumble, I will never again eat meat, lest I make my brother stumble.

3. **1 Corinthians 10:23** All things are lawful for me, but not all things are helpful; all things are lawful for me, but not all things edify.

4. **1 Corinthians 10:31** Therefore, whether you eat or drink, or whatever you do, do all to the glory of God.

C. Profitability or Sufficiency

1. **Deuteronomy 6:1** Now this is the commandment, and these are the statutes and

judgments which the LORD your God has commanded to teach you, that you may observe them in the land which you are crossing over to possess.

2. **Psalm 119:11** Your word I have hidden in my heart, that I might not sin against You.

3. **Psalm 119:97–100** Oh, how I love Your law! It is my meditation all the day. You, through Your commandments, make me wiser than my enemies; for they are ever with me. I have more understanding than all my teachers, for your testimonies are my meditation. I understand more than the ancients, because I keep your precepts.

4. **Psalm 119:105** Your word is a lamp to my feet and a light to my path.

5. **2 Timothy 3:16–17** All Scripture is given by inspiration of God, and is profitable for doctrine, for reproof, for correction, for instruction in righteousness, that the man of God may be complete, thoroughly equipped for every good work.

6. **Proverbs 5:18–19** rejoice with the wife of your youth. *As a* loving deer and a graceful doe, Let her breasts satisfy you at all times; And always be enraptured with her love.

II. **Regeneration:** The act of God whereby He puts to death the old sin nature in humans and generates entirely new life.

A. Assumes human inability

1. **Romans 1:18–32** And even as they did not like to retain God in *their* knowledge, God gave them over to a debased mind, to do those things which are not fitting…

2. **Ephesians 2:1–13** And you He made alive, who were dead in trespasses and sins, in which you once walked according to the course of this world, according to the prince of the power of the air, the spirit who now works in the sons of disobedience, among whom also we all once conducted ourselves in the lusts of our flesh, fulfilling the desires of the flesh and of the minds, and were by nature children of wrath, just as the others. But God, who is rich in mercy, because of His great love with which He loved us, even when we were dead in trespasses, made us alive together with Christ (by grace you have been saved), and raised us up together, and made us sit together in the heavenly places in Christ Jesus, that in the ages to come He might show the exceeding riches of His grace in His kindness toward us in

Christ Jesus. For by grace you have been saved through faith, and that not of yourselves; it is the gift of God, not of works, lest anyone should boast. For we are His workmanship, created in Christ Jesus for good works, which God prepared beforehand that we should walk in them. Therefore remember that you, once Gentiles in the flesh—who are called Uncircumcision by what is called the Circumcision made in the flesh by hands—that at that time you were without Christ, being aliens from the commonwealth of Israel and strangers from the covenants of promise, having no hope and without God in the world. But now in Christ Jesus you who once were far off have been brought near by the blood of Christ.

B. Posits an act of God on the spirit or soul of the inner man.

1. **John 3:3** Jesus answered and said to him, "most assuredly, I say to you, unless one is born again, he cannot see the kingdom of God."

2. **Titus 3:5** Not by works of righteousness which we have done, but according to His mercy He saved us, through the washing

of regeneration and renewing of the Holy Spirit.

3. **1 Peter 1:3** Blessed be the God and Father of our Lord Jesus Christ, who according to His abundant mercy has begotten us again to a living hope through the resurrection of Jesus Christ from the dead.

C. The old sinful nature is mortally wounded and the vigor of new life is infused.

1. **Romans 6:1-4** What shall we say then? Shall we continue in sin that grace may abound? Certainly not! How shall we who died to sin live any longer in it? Or do you not know that as many of us as were baptized into Christ Jesus were baptized into His death? Therefore we were buried with Him through baptism into death, that just as Christ was raised from the dead by the glory of the Father, even so we also should walk in newness of life.

2. **2 Corinthians 5:17** Therefore, if anyone is in Christ, he is a new creation; old things have passed away; behold, all things have become new.

D. The hardened heart is replaced by a soft heart inclined toward God.

1. **Jeremiah 31:33** But this is the covenant that I will make with the house of Israel after those days, says the LORD: I will put My law in their minds, and write it on their hearts; and I will be their God, and they shall be My people.

2. **1 Corinthians 3:2-3** I fed you with milk and not with solid food; for until now you were not able to receive it, and even now you are still not able; for you are still carnal. For where there are envy, strife, and divisions among you, are you not carnal, and behaving like mere men?

III. **Residence**: The Holy Spirit indwells every believer.
   A. The Promise of Jesus
   1. **John 14:15-18** If you love Me, keep My commandments. And I will pray the Father, and He will give you another Helper, that He may abide with you forever—the Spirit of truth, whom the world cannot receive, because it neither sees Him nor knows Him; but you know Him, for He dwells with you and will be in you. I will not leave you orphans; I will come to you.

   2. **John 14:25-27** These things I have spoken to you while being present with you. But the helper, the Holy Spirit, whom the Fa-

ther will send in My name, He will teach you all things, and bring to your remembrance all things that I said to you. Peace I leave with you, My peace I give to you; not as the world gives do I give to you. Let not your heart be troubled, neither let it be afraid.

3. **2 Corinthians 1:21–22** Now He who establishes us with you in Christ and has anointed us is God, who also has sealed us and given us the Spirit in our hearts as a guarantee.

B. The Temple of the Holy Spirit: **1 Corinthians 6:19** Or do you not know that your body is the temple of the Holy Spirit who is in you, whom you have from God, and you are not your own?

IV. **The Providence of God: Genesis 45:5.** But now, do not therefore be grieved or angry with yourselves because you sold me here; for God sent me before you to preserve life.

May I then conclude this exercise in the use of the concordance. If a Christian counselor is attempting to provide guidance for unbelievers, his task is only slightly less formidable than that of a secular counselor. God has given His counsel in the Bible, but the seed of the Gospel has until now fallen by the wayside, in stony places, or else thorns have choked it; so no impetus or power exists to make possible the life God intends. In this case the first and abiding objective must always be the New Birth.

Prayer as a Weapon for Good

We have observed that the Christian counselor is uniquely armed with the very Word of God, the regenerating experience of a changed heart, the permanently indwelling Holy Spirit of God as an internal guide and the revelation of God as given in Holy Scripture revealing to us the mind and purposes of God. There is, however, one concluding weapon in the Christian counselor's panoply of gracious and helpful weapons to assist in resolving the difficulties of counselors. That is prayer. Prayer is the God-ordained conduit through which His blessings flow and is seldom deployed in secular counseling. Here are some of the ways prayer functions. As B.H. Carroll noted, prayer is typical of the apparently feeble weapons that God employs:

> We see few fine tempered Damascus blades, but we see the sling of David, Gideon's pitchers and lamps, Shamgar's ox goad, the

jaw bone of an ass in the hand of Samson, and such like things, blessed of God to the pulling down of the strongholds of Satan and of the world. [40]

Carroll thus established prayer as a powerful weapon.

First, the Christian counselor admits his own inadequacies by seeking God's face before he ever begins. Our words can never resolve the manifold problems of needful souls that come to us. Before the counselor ever begins the session, he will want to ask that the Spirit of God will guide him to all truth as the session unfolds. Essential prerequisites include: asking that God will open the heart of the counselee, lead the counselor to understand the needs of the counselee correctly, and bring to mind the relevant Scripture that will meet these problems.

Second, in the midst of a counseling session, there often arises a situation in which the biblical counselor recognizes the arrival of the moment in which there is a special need for the touch of God. He may say to the counselee, "Brother John, I think God would like to hear from us about this. After all, only He can really bring healing to your mind in this regard. Would you kneel with me here and let us talk to God?"

---

40 B.H. Carroll, *Messages on Prayer* (Nashville, TN: Broadman, 1942), 43.

Then the counselor will pray. He may feel led at that point also to ask the counselee to pray. Hardly anyone fails to be blessed by hearing his name called in the presence of God. A healing solution often begins to develop right there.

Before a counselee departs, I love to give a written, spiritual prescription to those who come to me. Because I am convinced that many of the problems we face develop as a result of too much focus on the individual and an insufficient amount of attention on the needs of others, I love to give a personal prescription. The prescription will have a book I ask the person to read like *The Screwtape Letters* by C.S. Lewis. Then there will always be a few passages from the Bible to which I ask him to devote his attention. I often give one passage to read each day for ten days. Finally, I frequently suggest eight to ten items about which he is to pray. Some of these are for the needs of others. Occasionally, I even ask the counselee to become involved in providing for meeting some of these needs for others who are hurting.

In conclusion, I leave a few minutes between appointments so that I can prepare my mind, but also I can pray that God will significantly use my poor efforts to guide and bring a renewed mind to the counselee who just left the office. The prospect of being God's assistant in the counseling office brings a power to bear that no one else will harness. As E.M. Bounds pricelessly observed,

> What the Church needs today is not more machinery or better, not new organizations or more and novel methods, but men whom the Holy Ghost can use—men of prayer, men mighty in prayer. The Holy Ghost does not flow through methods, but through men. He does not come on machinery, but on men. He does not anoint plans, but men—men of prayer.[41]

In all other pastoral guidance scenarios, the believer is equipped with regeneration and the permanent indwelling of the Holy Spirit. It remains for the counselor to lead the counselee to the guidance of God provided in the Bible and encourage the counselee to trust the providences of an all-wise, all-knowing, enabling, just and loving heavenly Father to do always what is best for him. If Jerusalem has all of this to offer, how can Athens help? And more to the point, how can Vienna help?

---

41 Marion Price, *E.M. Bounds' Preacher and Prayer* (Asheville, NC: Revival Literature, 1998), 20.

Chapter 4

---◈---

Adversity:
God's University

To live is to encounter adversity. An index to success in life is an evaluation of one's response to adversity. For many, those reversals of life are not multiplied. Others are uniquely prepared to encounter such difficulties, but a significant part of the population is so sufficiently disturbed by these developments that they experience the need of some combination of counseling, pharmacological assistance, or even hospitalization. Biblical counselors as a rule generate no universal judgments about those suffering from such adversities, but they do insist that our adversities are properly understood as part of God's university. While we learn from good things that happen, the highest level of education occurs when difficulties arise. In the midst of these problems we learn of the grace and mercy of God, and we learn how to navigate the storms of life.

Biblical counseling declares that "men ought always to pray and not to faint" (Luke 18:1, KJV). The effectiveness of prayer unfolds at least on two levels. First, a close relationship with the Father is nurtured through walking daily with God. The most under-noticed declaration of the Great Commission is, "And look, I am with you every day until the designed climax of the ages" [author's translation] (Matt 28:20). The presence of Christ with the believer at every moment provides incredible perspective on life's adversities.

Second, prayer is the God-ordained conduit through which heavenly communication occurs. The problem is that so few people know how to pray. The disciples recognized this inadequacy, and that led to the request "Lord, teach us to pray" (Luke 11:1). Often the disciples of our Lord prayed, but they recognized that the quality of their prayer life was distinct from that of Jesus. Learning to walk with God in prayer is probably the most important single lesson that the counselor can impart. If the counselor has little walk with Christ in prayer, he has a limited arsenal with which to face the enemy of the soul. Teaching a counselee how to pray effectively may be the most effective counseling methodology that the counselor can provide!

The Nature of Adversities

The adversities of life may be placed in three broad categories. First, **adversities of opportunity**. Few people are content with failure or even apparent failure. However, almost all of us face some adversity in watching as some of our greatest hopes fail to materialize. As a youth, I envisioned myself as a great quarterback. What was lacking was only skill, size, speed, and opportunity. I played and loved football and basketball. Had my abilities been to be the "football," I might have experienced greater success. But the sad truth is that I was never the athlete that I dreamed of becoming. Somehow that failure was systematic of much of life for me. Thank God for the message of biblical counsel, which kept reminding me that finding and doing God's will for my life was all that mattered most to God.

One day, a biblically-based counselor asked me if I thought that Jeremiah was a success. I had read Jeremiah once but without much comprehension. I supposed he was successful, but by the time the counselor had walked me through Jeremiah's life, I was not so certain. The prophet faced adversities in his life and even in his calling to the prophetic ministry. My reflections changed when the counselor volunteered that Jeremiah had now been read and that his message had blessed the lives of people for over 2500 years!

Then the counselor asked, "Do you think you could handle that?"

My counselor, a layman in our church, helped me to believe that I was not wrong to have a dream, not in error to cradle a desire to succeed, and not a failure because most of those dreams never materialized. I would only be a failure if, unlike Jeremiah, I did not seek to know God's will and purpose or, as the Lord said to rebellious Saul, "It is hard for you to kick against the goads" (Acts 9:5). Success, he explained was not doing all the things about which I dreamed. Success was finding the will of God and completing that course.

From this experience I learned that many things about which I fantasized were not only unreasonable but also contrary to God's will. I also learned that patience, waiting on God to show His plan, added to diligent labor, would eventually establish God's purpose in my life. The importance of determining God's will is the reason for God's university.

Second, **adversities of health**. A long life inevitably presents physical challenges. These often occur in younger years. And as someone has wryly observed, "Life is one hundred per cent terminal." The death penalty has been assessed against the entire race. Understanding the effects of sin will do wonders for one's ability to deal with the tragic consequences. Nevertheless, the adversities of illness, physical challenges, and accidents are both devastating and real. A biblical counselor is armed with a plethora of examples and Scripture texts to buoy the spirits of any suffering ones who approach him.

First, it is never wrong to ask God to intervene; and, as the great physician, He can and often does bring healing. James 5 even provides a ceremony in which the sorrowing victim can bring all issues to the Holy Spirit. Selected passages, such as "Trophimus have I left sick in Miletus" (2 Tim. 4:20) facilitate the appropriate understanding that God's purpose does not always include immediate healing. The healing of the paralytic (Luke 5:17-26) focuses on the Lord's ability to heal and sometimes His will to do so. For those who are not miraculously healed, no passage matches Paul's comprehension of God's purpose as does 2 Cor 12:1-10. Here is a case where a malady develops at the direct action of the hand of God. The whole purpose of God is to induce humility and trust in Him and His plan. Furthermore, this thorn in the flesh is instructional. Paul learned more of the grace of God. He determined, therefore, to take pleasure in infirmities, and he grasped that in his weakness he actually discovered great strength. What counsel for those who suffer!

While I favor the practice of seeking God's face at the initiation and the conclusion of every counseling session, I wish to underscore the critical nature of prayer in behalf of the counselee's circumstances of illness and injury. Invoking an authority that transcends the finest human approaches is often profoundly comforting. Perfunctory prayer is not helpful. Heart-felt pouring out of the soul to God in personal intercession is the type of prayer that God will bless.

A final issue is **adversities of mental health**, one which plunges many believers and biblical counselors into near despair. A myriad of difficulties, disorders, and crises are not accounted for in the various issues of the DSM analysis. Even though not a sliver of actual science supports most of these conditions, even Christians frequently mistake these analyses as the product of "medical science" and defend them to the death. Yet as one New York psychiatrist said in a public discussion following a presentation I made, "Look, if the preacher claims success in assisting with the healing of drug addiction in only 50% of the cases of those who follow biblical directions, we need to abandon our failed methods and try his!" The important truth here is his honesty about the percent of failures in psychiatric medicine.

Once again, my purpose is not the denigration of the psychiatric industry, but rather to raise the question about why so many Christians adopt the atheistic world's psychiatric methods instead of trying the ways of Christ as offered in Holy Scripture. And why do ministers of Christ adopt the language and approaches of Freud and Skinner rather than the more effective methods and vocabulary of Jesus the Christ? Adversities of health are authentic and often devastating. But the cures of Christ are profound and educational.

ADVERSITIES OF PROVISION

Poverty and relative poverty are hard to stomach! Failure to accomplish certain educational goals has often proven so devastating that in places like Japan, the suicide rate is startlingly increasing. Then illusiveness of certain jobs, positions, and opportunities create uncertainty in human life. But poverty is not a pathogen that inevitably issues a disease. In the Scriptures an extraordinarily poor woman gave all she had–two mites, and Jesus said that she was a blessed woman (Luke 21:2-4). A widow made a cake for a prophet in the Old Testament and in her poverty received the blessings of God in that her vessel of oil never ran dry (1 Kings 17). Affluence appears to be accompanied by liabilities that often prove more devastating than poverty.

In any event, the biblical counselor knows that "a man's life does not consist in the abundance of things which he possesses" (Luke 12:15). The acquisition of wealth in the heavenly, and therefore permanent, realm is the joy that cannot be taken away. Lessons on the value of generosity, such as those mentioned above, abound in the Scriptures.

ADVERSITIES IN RELATIONSHIPS

By far the largest segment of adversity occurs in life in the midst of circumstances concerning interpersonal relationships. The first three categories mentioned above often contain elements of this. Marital problems and other mind-boggling challenges develop and extend to relationships with fellow workers, and people in every area of life and relationship. For our purposes here we might define an adversity in one's life as a circumstance of such magnitude that no matter what effort or money is expended, no exit from the circumstance of affliction ever appears. The situation seems hopeless.

As testimony to such developments, the story of Joseph is featured in the concluding chapters of Genesis. Abused by his eleven brothers, purchased as a slave by a caravan destined for Egypt, bought by Potiphar, falsely accused by Potiphar's wife, imprisoned where he was forgotten by those whom he helped, Joseph found himself in adversity he could not overcome by thought or physical prowess. His adversaries included family, government, and associates.

If Joseph had no means of conquering the adversity, he could and did elect not to despair but to use the circumstance as God's university. In return for his heartaches, sorrows, and disappointments, Joseph received a graduate education in what it means to have faith in God and the equivalent of a degree in circumstantial crisis counseling unparalleled in history. What a testimony from God's Word for a depressed, defeated, hopeless sojourner on life's highway!

A tragically short life is all that must be lived to realize that because of Satan and sin, life on this crowded planet will expose the traveler to temptation. For the same reasons life will open the traveler to abuse, misuse, injustice, and tragedy. Joseph's story is just one of the many biblical messages prepared for the counselee who no longer wishes to be a mere victim but wishes to become a conqueror.

The godly counselor knows that the Bible will direct us to heaven but delivers much more. God's Word not only directs us to the Savior's side but also explains the successful confrontation with all of life's problems along the way. The pilgrim is armed with spiritual weapons more effective than any weapon fashioned by mere mortals. Yes, our adversities are indeed in the university God employs to allow us to see the hand of God.

CHAPTER 5

Jesus' Amazing
Key to Wellness

A thoughtful counselor remains on alert with every
counselee that he hosts for the lurking, devastating presence of a serial thug roaming in the hearts of
a large number of troubled souls who seek his help.
That brusing adversary is unforgiveness. The failure to
forgive major and minor offenses stirs bitterness in the
heart. Bitterness is the slow-working poison that will
eventually snuff out the hope of God and eventually
the very life of the sufferer.

For Jesus' disciples, walking the commercial paths
of Galilee was a seminary education and an opportunity
to observe the life of a man whose intimate fellowship
with His Father was clearly the ideal that they themselves
coveted. Small wonder – none of these men, though
they prayed from birth, recognized the paucity of their

own prayer power. When the moment presented itself, they querried, "Lord, teach us to pray." As a significant conclusion to that prayer session, Jesus said to conclude the personal prayer by saying to the Father, "Forgive us our debts as we forgive our debtors." To this portion of the model prayer Jesus added this explanation, "For if you forgive men their trespasses, your Heavenly Father will forgive you. But if you do not forgive men their trespasses, neither will your Father forgive your trespasses" (Matt 6:14-15). This prayer places a premium on forgiveness. Clearly, if we expect forgiveness from God, we must provide forgiveness for others.

But what does it mean to forgive? *The Oxford English Dictionary* features a long discussion of "forgive" and its cognates. But it is closest to the New Testament when defining "forgives" as the act of ceasing to harbor resentment and wrath (*Oxford English Dictionary*, Vol. VI, p. 71). Understanding sin as a deliberate rejection of the plan and purpose of God, which generates disasters not only for the miscreant but also for others, and perhaps terminating in death, demonstrates the monumental step taken by Jesus to forgive anyone. Add to that the withering vocabulary of Greek words for sin, such as lawlessness, wickedness, transgression, missing the mark, and so forth; and one begins to grasp a focus on the nature and extent of what Jesus was determined to forgive.

On another occasion, Simon Peter apparently thought that he was being magnanimous when he suggested to Jesus that a man ought to exercise forgiveness toward another person an unbelievable seven times. "No," said the Master, "But until 70 times 7"! Psalm 78:38 affirms that forgiveness arises from a heart "full of compassion." Minus compassion there will be little forgiveness.

The agonizing moments of Christ's descent into the darkness of sin on the cross, as He was experiencing the initial pain of the nails, He called out to His Father in heaven, "Father, forgive them, for they do not know what they do" (Luke 23:34). Even men with wicked intent would have hesitated had they known that their Creator was the one toward whom they exhibited such cruelty. Jesus was followed later by Stephen, the first martyr of the church in asking forgiveness for even those who felt and acknowledged no guilt whatever (Acts 7:58). These set the ultimate example of forgiveness for all to follow.

Unforgiven actions on the part of humans leave victims with bitterness and not infrequently hatred in their hearts. Bitterness soon metastasizes in the soul, spreading like a cancer in the body. As the bodily disease ultimately disables its victim completely, so bitterness dislodges the joy of life. A significant number of those seeking counsel carry the weight of unforgiveness toward God, spouse, children, parents, fellow workers, or others. While the necessity of forgiveness may not be welcome news, this one act is more powerful than all the drug-induced cures for the sorrows of the soul.

David and Stephanie Palmer were enjoying a rare night in their Houston, Texas, home. David was a powerfully built man, while Stephanie was one of the most beautiful brides that I ever saw. Suddenly the door burst open and a stranger appeared with a shotgun in tow and malice in his soul. As he collected their valuables, the intruder thought Stephanie made a move to alert help. He discharged the shotgun directly in her face. Only by an act of God was Stephanie spared from instant death. What followed was more devastating than death. The disfiguring of Stephanie's face and the pain of more than a dozen surgeries made a temporary shipwreck of their lives. As anyone can imagine, no heartfelt discouragement was a stranger to Stephanie. As a powerful man, David experienced every response that anger and hurt could put together.

One day Stephanie surprised the world. She told her husband, "I want to get the message to that man who shot me that I forgive him. God loves him and will forgive him if he humbly seeks such forgiveness." On many occasions I have contemplated this amazing couple. I have observed them riding their motorcycles and laughing together through the countryside. I have querried my own heart: "Could I do that?"

The Palmers had a choice to make. Would they spend the remainder of their days on earth groaning and complaining as victims? Would they allow circumstances to triumph over the promises of God? Would they succumb to the bitterness of soul that normally encompasses the life of anyone in similar circumstances? Could they ignore the command of Christ to forgive? Would they find a way to dismiss the example of Jesus on the cross by arguing "But He was God"!

Through God's bountiful grace, my wife and I have lived to see 140 countries of the world and have met untold thousands of people. I sometimes speak of the Palmers; and when I do, I refer to them as the most beautiful couple that I ever knew! Not only their beauty reflected in their physical presence, but also their marriage and their spiritual life radiate the life and purpose of Christ as few I have ever observed. What the Palmers chose to do was not easy, but it was the grace of God mightily exhibited.[42]

Were we humans to master the art of forgiveness, the world would be a different place. First, the therapeutic offices of psychiatrists would forfeit one third or more of their patients. Second, exorbitant hospital and

---

42 This story is shared through special permission of Stephanie and David Palmer.

pharmaceutical bills would plummet. Third, gun-related violence would drastically subside. International conflicts and wars would decrease, saving thousands of lives. Perhaps, as important as any, churches would be full of "forgiven forgivers" whose examples of love and Christlikeness would permeate the scene.

First Corinthians 6 is home to the famous passage about which most Christians know– a prohibition against taking a brother to a court of law. However, as often as the passage is cited, the rationale seldom receives so much as an allusion. The prohibition assumes neither the guilt or innocence of either party in a matter of law. Instead, the passage asks in verse 7, "Why do you not rather accept wrong? Why do you not rather let yourselves be cheated?"

The apostle knows well that justice is often accomplished in a court of law, but sometimes it is not accomplished. Only God is a perfect Judge. Second, the church is the venue for disputes among believers. And far better is the act of suffering injustice and forgiving than creating upheaval in the church. Exercising forgiveness in such cases is God's way. Once again, the Joseph story in Genesis is one story of many that shows us the superiority of Christ's way.

CHAPTER 6

⚬————✦————⚬

Mechanical Addiction

Smartphones are not intrinsically wicked. A conglomeration of material substances and a unique product of human discovery, they are instruments of communication that all generations before us would have at least occasionally coveted. Like atomic energy, placed in evil hands, a smartphone can become an object of profligacy and destruction. The apparatus that enables a young man in America to call his ailing wife who is stranded in New Zealand and check on her condition also makes possible easy access to pornography of the most graphic variety that will sever the commitments in marriage and curtail his relationship with his Maker.

So, what does a biblical counselor say when a couple arrives and asks what to do about a teen with an intense addiction to playing games on a smartphone? The addiction is as real as substance abuse, and it has become obvious to the parents that serious harm to their child is developing in the wake of this malady. Recognizing that neither parent nor counselor is likely to resolve this issue, the biblical counselor assists the couple in learning how to seek the intervention of the Heavenly Father. Asking God to bring appealing objects and persons into the teen's life, pleading for divine wisdom for themselves, and interceding for God's powerful hand in the life of the teen are critical elements in the strategy.

Be sure that the parents know that some actions will almost certainly backfire. First, no good usually is accomplished by broadsides against the teen. Assessing the teen as useless, unproductive, evil, insensitive to parents or to God and so forth will most likely drive the teen deeper into his cave and make him inaccessible to anyone. Criticism and condemnation seldom effect healing.

On the other hand, to pretend that all is well and that there are no serious consequences to such a course of behavior will also prove counterproductive. Shrouded in a language of love, forgiveness, and confidence in the future, there are at least four points that must be carefully underscored. First, the present behavior of this teen will do tragic harm to him. Second, the behavior will eventually come home to roost in others whom he loves like his wife and his own children. Third, although his behavior will never quench the abundant love for him that bubbles to the surface in the hearts of his parents, this behavior, if it continues unabated, will crush the parents and introduce incredible grief into their lives. Finally, the teen must be informed that his Creator, the one who loves him more than anyone in the universe is displeased with this behavior. An appropriated biblical text such as Philippians 4:8-9 should reinforce this point.

Next, turn the negative into a positive. Acknowledge that the teen has succeeded in grasping considerable knowledge of electronic comprehension and suggest that the usefulness of this will depend on the expansion of this knowledge and the use of it to change the lives and fortunes of others. Consequently, you want him to study with master computer minds who will take him to incredible new vistas. Find a school, class, or at least an individual to help and enter a covenant with your teen. He pays half the cost through his own labor, and you provide the remainder. Remember, if he makes no sacrifice himself, he will consider the journey worthless. With this approach you are building on a commendation rather than belittling with a condemnation.

Actually, this problem is more profound than a mere addiction to video games. Your teenager has not developed a sufficiently well-rounded education. One of the earliest developments to protect the child is a love for reading. While you are late beginning a romance with the printed page, the key is locating books that will catch his fancy and captivate him. The list needs to be varied according to the interests of the child. The list attached here is not for everyone. It is typical of suggestions I would offer for a teen boy. Included is a heavy dose of good biographies along with a small number of carefully selected novels. The list includes fifteen incredible adventures from which your teen will profit profoundly.

- *Rhapsody in Black* by Richard Ellsworth Day (Literary Licensing)
- *Samuel Morris and the March of Faith* by Lindley Baldwin (Dimension Books)
- *Peace Child* by Don Richardson (Bethany House)
- *The River of Doubt* by Candice Millard (Random House)
- *Last of the Breed* by Louis L'Armour (Bantam)
- *Education of a Wandering Man* by Louis L'Armour (Bantam)
- *Mansfield's Book of Manly Men* by Stephen Mansfield (Thomas Nelson)
- *Here I Stand* by Roland Bainton (Hendrickson)
- *Arabian Sands* by Wilfred Thesiger (Penguin)

- *Into Thin Air* by John Krakaur (Villard)
- *The Professor and the Madman* by Simon Winchester (Harper)
- *Unbroken* by Lauren Hillenbrand (Random House)
- *The Daring Heart of David Livingstone* by Jay Milbrandt (Thomas Nelson)
- *The Anabaptist Story* by William Estep (Eerdmans)
- *Famous Conversions* by Hugh Kerr (Eerdmans)

The parent reads the book as the teen is reading. This provides material for discussion not only to determine that the young man is comprehending the assignment, but also the way is opened to spiritual discussion through the actions of the characters in the books. Once more, I want to stress the fact that this book list is for young men. Each parent needs to select his own list with a view to what may appeal to his teenager. But the books, secular and sacred, should not only appeal to the youth but also challenge her or him. Care should be taken that spiritual lessons should abound. Discussion is informal while driving, swimming, or pursuing another activity.

If a parent would assist his child, he must become a learner along with his teen. The conviction in the heart of a youth that he is on a team, pursuing something with his parent will limit the distance imposed by the passing of years and invigorate the parent-teacher as well. Learning together is also the object of journeys that are undertaken. At least three times a year, travel to a place that interests the teenager. But all journeys are study tours accompanied by appropriate reading and parent-offspring discussion.

Early on the youth needs to know that Mom and Dad do not always agree. Truthfully, he has known that since early childhood. But he should also know that Dad honors his wife as the reigning queen of the household and always treats her as the most precious possession God has given. And he needs to know that the queen recognizes and rejoices that Dad is the ultimate authority for the house and is definitely the spiritual leader. He is also the divinely appointed protector of the family. The process of extending the appropriate honor to both parents must be obvious to the teens.

Keep adding to your child's skills; and for every skill he masters, however insignificant, be generous in your commendations. These skill sets should vary from academic to things such as the playing of musical instruments to outdoor activities. By outdoor activities, I do not intend just hunting and fishing! I include such activities as the manicure of yards, cooking, and the upkeep of automobiles. A thousand times I have had occasion to wish my father had taught me basic mechanics and protocols for maintaining the automobile, and my son wishes that I had taught him. Work out regularly with your teen son. He cannot play video games when he is hoisting 200lbs. over his head. It will be good for you also, and do not forget to notice the ever-bulging biceps of your son!

As part of your son's outdoor training, make it a point to learn the names of all the animals of the field, the fish of the pond and of the ocean, the snakes and lizards, and consider scuba as something you can do together. Introduce him to the habitats and the habits of each animal. Preferably, while he names the dog, he also is the principal caretaker. Teach him or have him taught to train his own animal. If he learns that skill, he can pay his own way through college training dogs to basic obedience, guard and protection, obstacle course and other activities. This is a skill that is challenging, fun, and helpful. The happiest animals are always those with the most thorough training.

Find someone to whom your child becomes a minister. This person(s) can be old or young. I taught Tommy Maxwell, a future All-American to catch passes when he was ten years old, and I was probably 14 years old. We worked for hours. Maybe it will be an aged man whose house your son can paint or for whom he can make regular trips to the grocery store. But he needs a ministry! He needs responsibility by the time he is 13, and he needs that person(s) to be dependent on his faithfulness to the task.

Finally, walk closely by the side of your teenager in success and in failure! Standing with my quarterback son following a football game he lost was perhaps more important than standing by him when he won. Your teenager has to know that when he has failed, your love for him and admiration has grown stronger. He has to be conscious that your support for him is undeterred by defeat. When all others are gone, you will be there.

The summation of all this is that the assignment of parent is a tall order. The Bible makes clear that parenting while enjoyable, is expensive in terms of effort and time. Any rescue of your youth from the ravages of phone addiction involves few lectureships but rather extensive personal involvement and companionship. You are the key!

CHAPTER 7

——⋅⋅⟨∞⟩⋅⋅——

The Hallowed Explosive: Sexuality

Sexuality was God's idea. The union of one man and one woman emotionally and spiritually for a lifetime was the focus of His plan. His metaphor was that the man and woman entering this solemn covenant would become "one flesh."

Meeting the dawning of sexual awareness, in God's wonderful plan presented a method designed by God whereby one man could "know" one woman creatively and in a way that would produce happiness and productivity for this generation's young women and men a challenge that often seems to stagger adults. What do I do when my precious little girl announces that she was supposed to be a boy? What am I to do when my son announces that he prefers a sexual partner of the same gender? Maybe he wants a sex-change surgery?

Such is the environment in which Christians have the responsibility of rearing a family. Parenting is a magnificent journey, but no one suggests that it is easy.

Questions of human sexuality must be answered on the basis of God's purpose and plan in creation. Never has it been more essential to find out who you are and what you believe. If you define yourself as a believer in God (a theist) and if you believe that the Genesis account of origins is accurate, then the careful study of the first eleven chapters of Genesis is essential. You must then order your life and that of your family in a way that conforms to the truths taught in Genesis, following carefully the creation order designed by the Creator Himself.

But before venturing there, God begins with the parent. There are three necessary mandates. First, never find a way to call something "right" or even "O.K." that God has called "wrong." Second, regardless of what your offspring has done or expressed, your responsibility is to love him and constantly communicate that love to him. Christ did that for all of His creation by His death on the cross. Third, your own convictions must be as unchangeable as the oracles of God and yet they must be wrapped in the compassion of the Savior.

A reading of Genesis, especially the creation account leaves no doubt about important truths. First, since God created everything that partakes of "thing-ness," He is the creator of sexuality. Second, God in His graciousness created a way to perpetuate the race that simultaneously met additional needs in the human. In God's wonderful plan He designed marriage to be permanent – an unbreachable bond. In fact, God clearly states that He "hates divorce" (Mal 2:16). That experience of "sexual knowledge" described a relationship more intimate than the world would even understand. The husband and wife are to comfort one another. In Genesis 24:67, Isaac brought Rebekah into his mother Sarah's tent and "he was comforted by her." He did not have to seek the retreat of Sarah's tent in order to have tea with Rebekah. The human sexual experience for a husband and wife was to be a comforting respite from the exigencies of life, which would also serve as the means of perpetuating the race.

This concept of sexuality must be carefully taught in both home and church, and it must be broached relatively early in life. God, the creator, and artisan, who designed humans and all else that exists, is the one who hates or despises any other expression of human sexuality that deviates from His divinely established creation order. And He created them "male and female" (Gen 1:27). These concepts must all be transmitted quite early to Christian youth, and the message of Romans 1 must be carefully taught to children at an early age.

In addition, a healthy image of fatherhood and motherhood must be imparted to the child. The twin adventures of fatherhood and motherhood must be presented as an exciting endeavor that is blessed and honored by God. To use sexuality the way God designed it is to inherit the blessings of God. To do otherwise is to merit the judgment of God, intense unhappiness, and not infrequently diseases that often accompany such failure.

Younger teens need to read and discuss with parents basic genetics. This young science is graphic in describing the chromosomal structure of humans. Teens are often stunned to discover that all people have chromosomes. But males have two chromosomes that always have the pattern of one *x* chromosome and one *y*, while females have all *y* chromosomes. Despite what one does surgically, that divinely established pattern is unchangeable, indicating who God made you to be – either male or female. It cannot and will not change a human within.

Time spent with the teen and travel experience will often prove invaluable. The journey rafting the Grand Canyon with the Institute of Creation Research provides the opportunity to be away from ungodly influences while seeing the scientific evidence for the Flood of Noah and spending quality time for the parent and child. Travels with parents to other countries exploring history, culture, and people groups of the world can be intellectually stimulating and provide fun and fellowship as well. Hunting, fishing, scuba, and martial arts for young men are invaluable opportunities to learn about God's world of nature. Cooking, dog training, advanced computer studies are all invaluable to focus the youth on useful activities. Electronics, construction, the vast arena of the arts all provide constructive use of time to take the mind away from false or frivolous thinking. Exposure to the testimonies of great men and women who have faced the world's temptations and triumphed over them is one of the most important approaches and should not be overlooked or ignored.

Recognition by the parent that he is engaged in the fight of his life with the forces of evil is essential. Perfunctory prayer is not going to make the difference. But "the effectual, fervent prayer of the righteous man avails much" (James 5:16). The battle for the soul of your teenager will not be successful based on human ingenuity or clever counsel. If it is won, the Lord must intervene. The prayers of many must become the major weapon.

CHAPTER 8

———❦———

Regaining a
Critical Ministry

AD 63 dawned ominously for the apostle Paul. He was joined in his dark, vermin-filled prison by murderers and political dissidents—desperate men who had few regrets for the mayhem and murder they had committed. His own alleged guilt was based upon the fact that he followed a peripatetic rabbi who went about doing good. He was known as Jesus of Galilee. For Saul of Tarsus, Roman citizenship was not relieving his suffering, and there was no Roman psychiatrist to whom he could appeal. But the man knew that if his thoughts turned too much inward and if he chronicled to himself all of his sorrows so that they became the focus of his misery, he would crawl like a hunted animal into his cocoon. Or else he would be propelled by anger into an ill-advised confrontation with authorities, jailers, or inmates and in so doing probably forfeit his life. Instead, Paul chose to spend every moment concerned about the lives of his fellow inmates, whose lives were in disarray.

"Paul, I cannot believe this, but you have a visitor," chimed the bailiff. "He says his name is Onesimus, and he knows you from Colossae." Onesimus? The slave of Philemon? What could he be doing in Rome? "Yes," Paul replied, "may I speak with him?" The meeting was incongruous. Onesimus had recognized Paul when he saw him chained on a work detail in the Forum. [We actually have no clue as to how Onesimus found Paul. But the context suggests that some meeting like this must have transpired.] A sober meeting ensued. Paul was unsure what the future held for Onesimus, but his confidence in the providence of God was all encompassing.

But why was Onesimus in Rome? He had bolted. He was now a run-away slave who carefully concealed the sure marks of his owner. Distraught, he was now a fugitive. With only the small amount of money he had pilfered, the future he had imagined in Rome had turned to Sahara sand. Paul, though incarcerated at the moment, viewed a frightened Onesimus, from the perspective of a free Roman. Onesimus was a young man who wanted to be free. Paul identified with that and wished to help. Do you suppose that Paul's proposal was for Onesimus to spend some time with a platonic psychiatrist? Paul knew a man who could help. And after a few sessions with the platonic psychiatrist, perhaps Paul would arrange for a Roman government social worker to assist him in adjusting to the new social order. What possible defense could confessing Christian Philemon mount for owning slaves? Afterward Paul might seek out his own counselor to walk him through reversals of his prison experience.

That far-fetched scenario is not only false, but also there were no psychiatrists or social workers in Rome! Instead, I suspect their conversation proceeded something like this. "Onesimus, you should not have run away. But God has determined to make temples to Himself out of the battered tents of the lives of His children. I do not believe that God led you to do wrong, but I believe that He arranged this meeting today for your future."

Then Paul shared the way of Christ. According to verse 10 of Philemon, Onesimus responded to the adequacy of Christ for all human needs and believed in Jesus. While longing to keep Onesimus nearby to assist him, Paul knew that he must send him back to Philemon. This Paul did with a letter to Philemon making clear that Onesimus should be received back not as a slave but as a beloved brother (verse 16). Whether I am considering Paul, Onesimus, or Philemon, I so rejoice that the Church of the Lord Jesus had not abandoned its vision for pastoral ministry. I fear that much of this story would need to be rewritten in today's hyper-psychological cosmos. How does the church recover the transforming vision that turned a slave and his slave owner into two brothers?

The Great Commission of Jesus called for three activities in the church. These do not constitute all to which the church should devote its attention. But the three activities do provide a summation of what Jesus considered critically important for His disciples. They were to devote themselves to introducing others to Christ, to baptize them as a public witness to Christ, and to teach them all that Jesus taught. All of this was to be undergirded by fervent prayer for God's intervention.

Only a believer can do this. The finest secular counselor in the earth cannot lead people to Christ if he himself is not a believer. Neither can he teach his counselee what Jesus taught. In fact, if he is truthful, he has no desire to do any such thing. Jesus said, "I am the way, the truth, and the life" (John 14:6). Now get this one resounding note! Either Jesus is all of that, or He prevaricated in the most egregious manner. He either told the truth or He lied. You cannot have it both ways. Every local church needs to make up its mind which is true. If Christ and His way is life, then you must develop a genuine pastoral teaching/counseling ministry.

There is no necessity to be harshly critical of the psychological industry. And you must be rejoicing with every soul who is genuinely and permanently made better. Neither should you assume a role for which you are not certified. But if Jesus is the "Life," you must be exceedingly vocal, sweetly and gently aggressive, and more consistent than "Old Faithful" in making certain that no one misses the way of Christ. The predicament of Onesimus had a plethora of rough edges. All kinds of harm could have ensued. But God had a plan and a purpose in it all.

Followers of Christ, you simply must overcome the intimidation of "professional," "doctoral degree," "experts," and "authorities." There is an honor due all of that, and the Christian must always so acknowledge. That said, the second an "authority" contradicts God's Word, his best thought—if straying from Jesus' Way—must be kindly but flatly rejected. Is Jesus the Way, the Truth, and the Life, or is He a liar? You cannot avoid this dilemma. Sigmund Freud knew that. Why is it so difficult for the church to get it?

Second, churches must affirm once again that Christ's Way is hopelessly at odds with the world's way. Jesus said,

> If the world hates you, you know that it hat-
> ed Me before *it hated* you. If you were of

the world, the world would love its own. Yet because you are not of the world, but I chose you out of the world, therefore the world hates you" (John 15:18-19).

For example, Jesus says, "Love your enemies (Matt 5:44)." Is this a common piece of psychiatric advice? No—hardly ever, not because it does not work but because there are distinctly Christian reasons for this command.

Third, call your church to ardent prayer that God will open the way and profoundly bless the pastoral counseling ministry. Say cordially to people, "Look, I am not a licensed professional counselor. I am a person who has studied and committed to memory the way of Christ. I can help you find that way if this is your desire." Word gets around town quickly that you are sharing something that really works. And people will come. But much of your success in every way depends on the intervention of God. Consequently, prayer is most often the missing element. Its absence makes any chance of success obsolete.

Is there a distinction to be made between preaching/teaching on one hand and counseling on the other? As it concerns content, we may be confident that there is little if any difference. The difference between preaching/teaching and biblical counseling is one of circumstance. The transfer of life-transforming information initiated by the personal evangelist or minister is a cherished freedom in America, and there should be no hesitancy on the part of the preacher, teacher, or evangelist to embark on that discussion. But if a troubled individual approaches the biblical counselor, the circumstances are different though the instruction and guidance remain the same. Consequently, seemingly to me in the present milieu, full disclosure is essential. The biblical counselor might suggest, "While I'm happy to converse with you about this problem, I must ask that you understand that I am not a licensed professional counselor, and I do not dispense pharmaceutical medications of any variety. My approach to the difficulties of life is to discover and to follow the teachings of God's Word in the Bible. My aim is to find and follow God's will and purpose for all things."

This disclaimer is true. Often the prospective counselee will be undeterred, perhaps having already tried traditional therapeutic approaches and discovered them to be ineffective. Many want to know what God thinks and receive His solution as an answer to the problem faced. Total honesty coupled with unapologetic certainty is the role of the "biblical" counselor.

A "biblical" counselor must be a master of two things: He must know what the gospel is, and he must be able to present the claims of Christ in the most lucid and helpful fashion. Furthermore, he must have and grasp biblical instruction on all the major issues of life. He must be aware of the Scriptures addressing love, forgiveness, faith, God's providence, human sexuality, gender, child development, victory, defeat, and numerous other prevalent topics.

A mandatory skill is that of "listening." Seasoned counselors have long since learned that the counselee may not lead with the whole problem or may not even understand the nature of the real issue. Asking appropriate questions and giving careful attentiveness to answers from the counselee is mandatory for a Christian counselor. Remember that ideas such as forgiveness, returning good for evil, and loving your enemy, while fairly well-known, are as foreign to most fallen humans as a pet ardvark.

Other than a cordial handshake as a greeting, remember not to touch the counselee. Be circumspect in all relationships with the counselor giving no opportunity for the counselee or any other person to take offense. Remember to incorporate a third party (usually the spouse) with any member of the opposite gender.

Finally, employ the agency of prayer, which has therapeutic value surpassing all human wisdom. Pray privately before beginning a counseling session. You cannot hope to be successful in biblical counseling without the guidance and insight of the Holy Spirit. In the midst of the session, seek God's face. When faced with vexing problems or struggling with misunderstanding, a journey to the throne of grace is irreplaceable. At the conclusion of the session, prayer underscores the fact that the counselee does not face these issues alone. God wants him to live a confident, vibrant faith walk with God; and hopefully you have shown him how this can happen.

The method of biblical counseling is not difficult or complicated. Love and compassion are required. Patience is a great asset. A well-developed sense of humor is a treasure. Even with all of that, if you fly solo, you will not succeed. Only on the wings of the Spirit of God can counselors assist in the deepest needs of human existence. That news is not a negative, however. To the contrary, the believer approaches the task of counseling with the promise of the superintendence of the living God.

Appendix 1

Annotated Bibliography
of Essential Books

Breggin, Peter R. *Toxic Psychiatry: Why Therapy, Empathy, and Love Must Replace the Drugs, Electroshock, and Biochemical Theories of the "New Psychiatry."* New York: St. Martin's Press, 1991.

This former teaching fellow at Harvard Medical School and long-time consultant with the National Institute of Mental Health for years has been sounding in his writings a warning about psychiatric treatment and the use of medications and their value or harm. This text is one of many and accompanies a voluminous website found at *www.breggin.com*.

Carlat, Daniel J. *Unhinged: The Trouble with Psychiatry—A Doctor's Revelations about a Profession in Crisis.* New York: Free Press, 2010.

> Carlat, a Harvard-trained psychiatrist, reveals the risks of the "popular" psychiatric diagnoses and the "cocktails" of medications that are prescribed to treat them. He also reveals the inner workings of "collusion" between psychiatrists and drug companies.

Dineen, Tana. *Manufacturing Victims: What the Psychology Industry is Doing to People.* Montreal, QC: Robert Davies Multimedia, 2001.

> Everyone is a victim. The public has a broad awareness of this problem in psychology, but the extent of the difficulty is made evident in Dineen's book, an essential read. Both causes and consequences of the effects of "victimology" are elucidated by Dineen.

Frances, Allen. *Saving Normal: An Insider's Revolt against Out-Of-Control Psychiatric Diagnosis, DSM-5, Big Pharma, and the Medicalization of Ordinary Life.* New York: HarperCollins, 2013.

The former Chair of the DSM-4 committee reveals how the new edition of the DSM will turn our current diagnostic inflation into hyperinflation by converting millions of "normal" people into "mental patients." In addition, Frances gives a historical review of "psychiatric fads" that have driven treatment.

Glenmullen, Joseph. *Prozac Backlash: Overcoming the Dangers of Prozac, Zoloft, Paxil, and Other Antidepressants with Safe, Effective Alternatives.* New York: Simon and Schuster, 2000.

At the time of publication, Glenmullen was a clinical instructor in psychiatry at Harvard Medical School. In this text, Glenmullen calls into question the overuse of psychiatric medications and the useful alternative treatments that bring questions to the standard understanding of the etiology of the diagnoses.

Gotzsche, Peter C. *Deadly Medicines and Organized Crime: How big pharma has corrupted healthcare.* London: Radcliffe Publishing, 2013.

Gotzsche attempts to expose the pharmaceutical industries and their "charade of fraudulent behavior, both in research and marketing where the morally repugnant disregard for human lives is the norm." His effort is to reveal the truth behind efforts to confuse and distract the public and their politicians.

Greenberg, Gary. *The Book of Woe: The DSM and the Unmaking of Psychiatry*. New York: Blue Rider Press, 2013.

Greenberg reveals the history of the growth, size, and influence of the DSM. His thesis is to demonstrate how the use of this manual turns suffering into a commodity and the APA into its own biggest beneficiary.

Kirsch, Irving. *The Emperor's New Drugs: Exploding the Antidepressant Myth*. New York: Basic Books, 2010.

Kirsch reveals how he spent years referring patients to psychiatrists to have their depression treated with drugs. However, with 15 years of research, he demonstrates that what everyone "knew" about antidepressants is wrong—what the medical community considered a cornerstone of psychiatric treatment is little more than a faulty consensus.

Milton, Joyce. *The Road to Malpsychia: Humanistic Psychology and our Discontents.* San Francisco: Encounter Books, 2002.

> Impatient with human limitations, intent of putting the self at the center of the universe, the humanistic psychology movement was momentarily triumphant. But as Joyce Milton reveals, the movement's questing selves eventually created a culture of narcissism; the new values were exposed as clichés in disguise; and the gospel of self-esteem dwindled into psychobabble.

Moncrief, Joanna. *The Bitterest Pills: The Troubling Story of Antipsychotic Drugs.* London: Palgrave Macmillan, 2013.

> Senior Lecturer in the Department of Mental Health Sciences at University College London and practicing psychiatrist Joanna Moncrieff challenges the accepted account that portrays antipsychotics as specific treatments that target an underlying disease or chemical imbalance.

Moncrief, Joanna. *The Myth of the Chemical Cure: A Critique of Psychiatric Drug Treatment*, rev. ed. London: Palgrave Macmillan, 2009.

Moncrieff attempts to expose the view that psychiatric drugs target underlying diseases as a fraud. She traces this view historically and suggests that it was adopted, not because there was evidence to support the view but because it served the interests of the psychiatric profession.

Peele, Stanton. *Diseasing of America: Addiction Treatment out of Control*. Lexington: Lexington Books, 1989.

Peele documents the scientific fallacies of the "addiction-as-disease" movement. In his view, the disease model sets up the sufferer for future irresponsibility, which leads to relapse and retards personal growth.

Speed, Ewen, Joanna Moncrieff, and Mark Rapley, eds. *De-Medicalizing Misery II: Society, Politics and the Mental Health Industry*. London: Palgrave Macmillan, 2014.

The editors attempt to demonstrate faulty thinking in the contemporary mental health landscape and to pose possible solutions to the continuing problem of emotional distress and disturbance.

Szasz, Thomas S. *The Myth of Mental Illness: Foundations of a Theory of Personal Conduct.* New York: Dell Publishing, 1961.

In this 50+-year-old text, Szasz reveals a theory of human conduct in which mental diseases do not exist in the sense in which bodily diseases exist, and man is considered to be always responsible for his acts. At the time of writing, his thesis seemed odd and controversial to many, but in light of the other texts in the bibliography, his writing is timely.

Taylor, Michael Alan. *Hippocrates Cried: The Decline of American Psychiatry.* New York: Oxford University, 2013.

This internationally-known neuropsychiatrist argues that the mentally ill are no longer receiving the care they need. He details how psychiatrists rely too heavily on the DSM, and how it neglects important conditions and symptoms, which leads to an improper diagnosis of patients' conditions.

Whitaker, Robert. *Anatomy of an Epidemic: Magic Bullets, Psychiatric Drugs, and the Astonishing Rise of*

Mental Illness in America. New York: Broadway Books, 2010.

Science and history writer Robert Whitaker investigates a medical mystery: Why has the number of mentally ill dramatically increased over the past two decades? The author reveals how other societies have begun to alter their use of psychiatric medications and are now reporting much improved outcomes. His question is: Why can't such a change happen in the United States?

This annotated bibliography, demonstrating among other things the extent of the questions arising within the psychotherapeutic and pharmacological communities about the usefulness and integrity of the enterprise, was prepared by Dr. Frank Catanzaro, Adults Pastor at Grace Baptist Church in Knoxville, Tennessee. I am especially grateful for his contribution.

Appendix 2

———◆∞◆———

Biblical Counseling Agreement

I, the undersigned over the age of 18, acknowledge that I am seeking Biblical counseling not healthcare counseling that is offered by state licensed healthcare professionals. I further acknowledge that I understand that the counseling I will receive will be based on the Bible and its application. I understand that I have been told that if my situation improves or is cured by following Biblical counseling, the Lord has done this, not the one providing me Biblical counseling. I freely sign this agreement after reading and understanding it.

Signed this ____day of _____,

_____

*Adapted from form prepared by Shelby Sharpe.

Printed in the USA
CPSIA information can be obtained
at www.ICGtesting.com
CBHW021648201223
2699CB00004B/15